Collins

WATERWAY

Norfolk Broads

Introduction	2	Waterways Signs and Journey Times	34
Getting Onto the Water	4	Key to Map Pages	36
Boating Need to Know	8	Broads Mapping	38
Navigation Notes	14	Where to Hire	70
Stay Safe	18	Wildlife of the Broads	76
Other Activities	20	Places to Visit	86
Where to Get More Information	24	Acknowledgements	95
Eating Out	28	Index	96

Published by Nicholson
An imprint of HarperCollins Publishers
Westerhill Road, Bishopbriggs, Glasgow G64 2QT
www.harpercollins.co.uk

First published by Nicholson 2010
New edition published by Nicholson 2012, 2014, 2018

© HarperCollins Publishers Ltd 2018

Researched and Edited by Cicely Oliver, David Lobban,
Judith Pile and Jonathan Mosse.

Wildlife text from *Collins Complete Guide to British Wildlife*
and *Collins Wild Guide*.

A catalogue record for this book is available from
the British Library

Printed in China by RR Donnelley APS Co Ltd

ISBN 978-0-00-825800-9

10 9 8 7 6 5

This product uses map data licensed from Ordnance Survey
© Crown copyright and database rights (2017)
Ordnance Survey (100018598)

The representation in this publication of a road, track or path
is no evidence of the existence of a right of way.

The publisher gratefully acknowledges the assistance given by
the Broads Authority in the preparation of this guide, in particular
Lucy Burchnall, Jess Tunstall, Steve Fairbrass, Jon Hopes, Adrian
Clarke, Steve Birtles and the Broads Authority Rangers. Thanks are
also due to CAMRA representatives and branch members.

MIX
Paper from
responsible sources
FSC www.fsc.org
FSC™ C007454

This book is produced from independently certified FSC™ paper
to ensure responsible forest management.

For more information visit: www.harpercollins.co.uk/green

■ INTRODUCTION

The Broads (the Norfolk and Suffolk Broads) are one of Britain's best-known holiday boating areas. They make up Britain's largest and most important protected wetland and are a national park providing a home to some of the rarest plants and animals in the country. A unique and enchanting wetland, with over 200 km (125 miles) of lock-free, navigable tidal waters, all waiting to be explored.

The area extends over the lower reaches of the Rivers Waveney, Yare and Bure, together with the Rivers Ant and Thurne (tributaries of the Bure) and the River Chet (the tributary of the Yare). The low-lying, wetland landscape contains around 60 shallow lakes. These lakes are referred to as 'broads', while we use the term 'the Broads' to refer to the entire area.

The history of the familiar landscape we see today dates back to the Middle Ages in the form of written evidence of peat digging in the Broads. By this time, much of the area had been cleared of woodland for fuel and building material. In the 12th century peat digging had become a major industry, the cut turfs being used for fuel. Almost every Broads settlement had its own pit, from where the peat was extracted on a huge scale. Gradually sea levels rose and the pits flooded making cutting more difficult until, by the 14th century, the peat diggings were abandoned.

For a long time, the origins of the broads were not properly understood. In 1952 Dr J M Lambert advanced the theory that these waterways were, in fact, man-made: a suggestion received with scepticism. However, researchers discovered that the sides of the broads were vertical, not gently sloping as would be the case with a naturally formed lake: evidence that these immense areas of water had originally been dug by hand. This was supported by the knowledge that there had been a massive demand for peat in the area, which by the 14th century was both densely populated and prosperous.

Historically, the Broads' economy was centred on agriculture and the profitable wool trade. The marshman's way of life exploited the natural landscape of the lowland river valleys by tending cattle, cutting reeds, building dykes and drainage mills, harvesting fish and hunting wildfowl.

In the 16th century, Norwich, after London, was the second largest city in England, its wealth built on wool, weaving, fishing, agriculture and general trade. There was a large export market from Norwich via Great Yarmouth and the waterways – natural and man-made – were major trading routes essential for communication and commerce, not only for meeting the large market for goods outside the area but for local communication supplying the riverside settlements.

The distinctive Norfolk wherries (*see* page 5 for a brief description) were developed to navigate this area of rivers and lakes, and for several hundred years provided essential transport. The coming of the railways in the 1870s started the decline in commercial sailing, as the area's transport system was developed and cargo-carrying was transferred to the trains. However, the railways also opened up the Broads to recreation and enterprising wherry owners converted their vessels to accommodate passengers in order to make up lost income. Inhabitants of the Broads had always used the waterways for pleasure, alongside their day-to-day work and these early wherry conversions were the start of the tourism business that has continued to expand over the years and now sees around seven million visitors enjoying the Broads annually.

However, the ensuing decades of increasing visitor numbers, boating and intensive agriculture had a detrimental effect on the fragile environment of this area. By the 1950s the clear Broads water had become cloudy and polluted, the river banks were eroding and the unmanaged fenland was turning into scrub. After alarming reports on the degradation of the Broads, the original Broads Authority was created in 1978 to manage the area.

Following considerable success in dealing with the environmental problems and tackling restoration, the 1988 Broads Act gave status equivalent to a National Park, operating from 1989, one of 15 specially protected areas within the UK. The Broads National Park has three main aims: to conserve and enhance the natural beauty, wildlife and cultural heritage of the Broads; to promote opportunities for the understanding and enjoyment of the special qualities of the Broads by the public; to protect the interests of navigation. The National Park must have responsibility for the needs of agriculture and forestry and the economic and social interests of those who live or work in the Broads.

This guide is designed to help visitors plan their visit to the Broads in advance and to be a practical reference while exploring the area. For many people, the best way to discover the Broads is by boat and this book describes the varied ways in which you can get onto the water in all types of craft, whether for an hour's boat trip, for a week-long boating holiday, a day's canoeing or simply by hiring a rowing boat. Of course, not everyone wants to take to the water so we have also included lots of information for the casual visitor as well as those wishing to explore the area on foot or by bicycle, or to enjoy a day's fishing. There are also chapters listing places to eat and places to visit. The unique wildlife of the Broads is included too, with a chapter describing some of the plants and creatures that may be seen on land and in the water.

Please note that distances given are approximate and that conversions are rounded up to the nearest 0.5 km or mile.

Ted Ellis, one of Norfolk's best-loved naturalists and broadcasters, described the Broads as 'a breathing space for the cure of souls'. We hope that this guidebook will encourage you to explore the Broads, enjoy their unique atmosphere and special qualities, and to find your own breathing space.

If you would like to comment on any aspect of the guide, please write to Nicholson Waterways Guides, HarperCollins Publishers, Westerhill Road, Bishopbriggs, Glasgow G64 2QT or email nicholson@harpercollins.co.uk.

Whether you are an experienced sailor or are completely new to boating, the Broads will provide you with the perfect way of getting onto the water. Boats of all types, large and small, can be hired by the hour or day, for short breaks and for whole weeks.

The Broads Authority publishes *Code of Conduct* leaflets for canoeing, rowing, sailing and day boat cruising. The leaflets offer simple tips and information to help make your trip a safe and enjoyable experience.

BOAT HIRE

Please book a boating holiday from a licensed operator – only in this way can you be sure that you have proper insurance cover, service and support during your holiday. It is illegal for private boat owners to hire out their craft. The Broads Authority website *(www.broads-authority.gov.uk/ boating)* and their Information Centres provide information on hire companies. Take a look at the Where to Hire chapter of this guide *(see page 70)*, for a full list of what is available for hire, together with operators providing tuition. Extensive information and advice on booking a boating holiday is available from the Inland Waterways Association *(www.waterways.org.uk)*.

Full instruction is always provided when you hire any craft. Take notes, follow the boatyard's instructions and don't be afraid to ask if there is anything you do not understand. You could also consider signing up for a training course.

ELECTRIC BOATS

Electric boats are quiet and better for the environment than ordinary motor boats. They are available for hire and the Broads Authority also offers boat trips aboard electric boats.

CANOES

Paddling your own canoe is a unique way to get up close to nature. Canadian canoes can be hired from centres across the Broads. No previous experience is necessary and the canoes are suitable for families with children. Life-jackets are included in the hire price. Pre-planned itineraries and routes are available. New canoe trails and canoe hire centres can be found on *www. broads-authority.gov.uk/boating/canoeing*. The British Canoe Union *(www.bcu.org.uk)* can provide details of training courses for beginners.

MOTOR BOATS

Motor boats to suit everyone from couples to large families can be hired from the many hire centres and boatyards around

Hire boats and crusiers come in many shapes and sizes.

the Broads. All the necessary safety equipment is included in the price of hire, together with on-board facilities ranging from the basic to the luxurious.

SAILING YACHTS AND DINGHIES
Don't let a lack of experience put you off having a go at sailing. If you have a little experience – even in the smallest dinghy – you will quickly learn to handle a sailing cruiser, and, as with all types of boat hire, full instruction will be provided. Several boatyards around the Broads offer trips with qualified skippers.

WINDSURFING
The best places to launch are at Oulton Broad (page 66) and the purpose-built beach at Hickling Broad (page 40) where a small fee is charged. Courses are available at Whitlingham Adventure (page 74).

SAILING SCHOOLS
Even if you have no sailing experience at all, various centres offer expert tuition in sailing, canoeing and windsurfing. The generally quiet waters of the Broads are an ideal area in which to learn to handle a sailing boat and you can concentrate on the art of sailing without worrying about navigation. The chapter Where to Hire (*see* page 70) lists organisations and boat yards offering tuition within the Broads area. The Royal Yachting Association offers accredited courses all over the country. These include tuition in small and large boat sailing, motor cruising and windsurfing. Visit their website (*www.rya.org.uk*) for more details.

BOAT TRIPS
If you are not hiring your own boat, many places offer boat trips and guided tours of the Broads. The Broads Authority operates several electric boat trips, allowing you to explore some of the most beautiful nature reserves in the area. It is advisable to book these trips in advance. For a full list of boat trips, *see* Where to Hire, page 70, *See also* Places to Visit, page 95

Electric Eel **Wildlife Water Trail**
(page 44) *Near Ludham, Great Yarmouth, Norfolk NR29 5PG (01692 678763; www.enjoythebroads.com).* Explore How Hill National Nature Reserve on an Edwardian-style electric boat. Telephone to book. *See also* Places to Visit, page 92.

Liana (page 42) *Hoveton Riverside Park. Book at Hoveton Information Centre, Station Road, Noveton, Norfolk NR12 8UR (01603 756097/782281; hovetontic@broads-authority.gov.uk).* An Edwardian-style electric launch which takes you along the River Bure towards Coltshill and back.

Ra (page 50) *Whitlingham Country Park, Whitlingham Lane, Trowse, Norwich, Norfolk NR14 8TR (01603 756094/617332; whitlinghamtic@broads-authority.gov.uk).* Britain's first solar-powered passenger boat, named after the Egyptian sun god, takes visitors (including wheelchair users) around Whitlingham Great Broad. *See also* Places to Visit, page 95.

The Lady Ann (page 41) *Horsey Staithe, Norfolk NR29 4EF (07791 526440; www.wildlifeboattrips.co.uk)* Ross' hour long wildlife boat trips from Horsey Staithe. The Lady Ann is a classic wooden boat, stable and perfect for viewing the unique wildlife and history of Horsey Mere SSSI.

The Norfolk Wildlife Trust runs regular trips by electric boat on Hickling Broad (page 40; *01692 598276 to book*) and Ranworth Broad (page 43; *01603 270479 to book*). *See also* Places to Visit, page 91.

NORFOLK WHERRIES
The Norfolk Wherry was a trading sailing craft which evolved to suit the particular conditions encountered on the Broads. It was highly manoeuvrable and could operate under most conditions. The mast was built to a special design, pivoting and counter-balanced by an enormous metal weight, which meant that it could be lowered quickly when passing under bridges. Cargoes of every description were carried in these boats until the building of railways

and roads eclipsed their use.
Several wherries have been restored and are available for charter (*see* below).

Wherry Maud Trust The trust was established in 2015 to take over the operation of the wherry Maud. Trip are arranged regularly by the Trust, visit *www.wherrymaudtrust.org.*

Norfolk Wherry Trust (page 44) *Forsythe Wherry Yard, Horsefen Road, Ludham, Norfolk NR29 5QG (01508 580402; www.wherryalbioncom).*

Wherry Yacht Charter *The Wherry Base, Barton House, Hartwell Road, Wroxham, Norfolk NR12 8TL (01603 781474; www.wherryyachtcharter.org).* A charitable trust which has half the Broads wherries for charter. *See also* Where to Hire, page 72.

USING YOUR OWN CRAFT
Slipways and launch sites
There are public slipways at Beccles (page 65; *01502 712225*), Hickling Staithe (page 40), Horning (page 43; *01692 630434*), Horstead (page 42), Hoveton Riverside Park (page 42), Oulton Broad Yacht Station (*01502 574946*) and the Water Sports Centre (*01502 587163*) both on page 67, Pug Lane Staithe at Repps with Bastwick (page 45), Smallburgh Staithe at Wayford Bridge (page 39), Sutton Staithe (page 39), Cantley (page 58) and South Walsham (page 44).

Some boatyards have slipways which can be used for a small charge (a list is available from the Broads Authority and on its website). It is always advisable to telephone and confirm availability in advance.

Tolls and craft registration
Any vessel kept or used within the Broads Authority navigation area for more than 28

Rowing boats tied up at Filby Broad near Great Yarmouth.

days must be registered with the Authority, carry third party insurance and have paid the appropriate annual toll. Annual tolls can be paid through the Broads Authority main office.

Short visit tolls are available for periods of up to 28 days. All Broads Authority Information Centres and some yacht stations and boatyards issue short visit tolls. Craft registration is free and available from the Broads Authority main office, or visit their website.

National Boat Safety Scheme

The Broads Authority operates the Boat Safety Scheme (BSS). This comprises essential safety requirements and is jointly managed by Canal and River Trust and the Environment Agency, and administered through the Boat Safety Scheme office. Full information and *The Boat Safety Scheme Essential Guide* are available from the Broads Authority main office or direct from the Boat Safety Scheme, *First Floor*

North, Station House, 500 Elder Gate, Milton Keynes, Buckinghamshire MK9 1BB (0333 202 1000; www.boatsafetyscheme.org). The website also offers useful advice on preventing fires and avoiding carbon monoxide poisoning.

A Boat Safety Certificate (for new boats, a Declaration of Conformity) is required by all craft with engines and/or with heating, lighting, cooking, refrigeration and other domestic appliances. It does not apply to open vessels solely propelled by an outboard motor as long as the vessel does not have any of the above facilities or appliances, and does not carry fuel other than that solely for use of powering the outboard motor.

Boats may visit the Broads navigation area for up to 28 days per year, on not more than four separate occasions, without the need to submit a valid BSS certificate to the Authority. Visiting boats will be subject to a random Dangerous Boat Check.

Getting Onto the Water

This chapter provides advice and information on various aspects of boating on the Broads. In all cases, further details – including up-to-date lists of facilities and the series of *Waterways Code* leaflets – can be obtained from the Broads Authority main office, their Information Centres and website. For contact details, *see* Where to Get More Information, page 24.

The Broads Authority has produced a series of videos, which contain lots of practical boat handling and navigation advice, as well as visitor and environmental information.They are particularly useful to those new to boating, The videos are available to watch online *(www. broads-authority.gov.uk/boating/navigating-the-broads/boating-beginners)*.

The Boater's Handbook is a booklet produced jointly by Canal and River Trust and The Environment Agency and contains an introduction to basic boat handling and safety information. It is available to download free of charge from *www. canalrivertrust.org.uk/boating/navigating-the-waterways/boaters-handbook* and *www. environment-agency.gov.uk*.

BOAT HANDLING

If you are hiring a boat, your boatyard will brief you thoroughly on the various controls, boat handling and manoeuvring, and mooring. You will also be provided with a *Skipper's Guide* for ready reference while you are onboard.

- A cruiser is big and heavy and has no brakes. To stop it you must put it into reverse – it can take a long time to stop, so you must think and plan ahead.
- The water in a river or broad is always moving. The water and your boat will be affected by the winds and tides. Be aware that steering straight may not keep you on a straight path.
- Steering a boat with a rudder is different from steering a car. The boat pivots on its centre point and it is the bow (front) and the stern (back) of the boat that move. You will be facing the bow, but always

think about what the back end of your boat is doing, to prevent it swinging out into other boats or the bank.

- Always manoeuvre the boat at slow speeds. You must be able to operate your boat without causing injury to people, wildlife, the environment, moorings, structures on the banks and other property.
- In general children under eight must not drive a motor boat. There are some circumstances in which children aged between eight and fourteen may drive a motor boat – visit *www.broads-authority. gov.uk* and check the Navigation Byelaws for details.
- Most boats turn better in one direction than another. When viewed from behind, most boats' propellers turn clockwise – these boats will turn better to port (left).

BOAT SAFETY SCHEME
See Getting Onto the Water, page 7.

BOATYARDS
Boatyards and other facilities are shown on the maps. Hire boaters should always contact their hire centre with any queries in the first instance.

Electric charging point.

Broads Authority Ranger on patrol on the River Waveney approaching Somerleyton Swing Bridge (page 66).

BROADS AUTHORITY RANGERS

The Rangers travel the Broads waterways in easily recognised boats. They enforce speed limits and carry out radar speed checks, and ensure that boats navigate properly. In addition, they are able to assist boaters with day-to-day issues including safety procedures, tidal conditions and planning.

BROADS CONTROL

Broads Control deals with everything to do with navigating the Broads and rivers, from routine enquiries to emergency liaison with the coastguard, police and the Environment Agency. During peak season the office gets busy, so please be patient and do use the answerphone provided. In the event of an emergency, dial *999* – the emergency services will always contact Broads Control as required. Contact Broads Control on *01603 756056* or email *broads.control@ broads-authority.gov.uk*.

ELECTRIC CHARGING POINTS

There are electric charging points at 20 locations throughout the Broads, on the rivers Ant, Bure, Chet, Thurne, Waveney, Wensum and Yare. They are indicated on the relevant mapping pages or by visiting *www.broads-authority.gov.uk/ boating/facilities*. The charging points not only enable electric boats to reliably travel throughout the Broads waterways, but allow the electricity supply on diesel powered boats to be topped up easily.

The charging pillars are straight forward to use and the charging cards are available from the Broads Authority head office, Broads Information Centres and other outlets close to the charging points.

EMERGENCIES

- Contact the emergency services by calling *999* for coastguard, fire, police or ambulance services. To contact the police on less urgent matters dial *101*.
- On a hire boat, contact details for your boatyard will be in your *Skipper's Handbook*.
- If you have to contact the emergency services or your boatyard, be as specific as possible about your location. Use the nearest Broads Authority 24 hour mooring as a reference to where you are – the name of the mooring is shown on the signs. Always try to keep track of where you are on the Broads.
- Keep your mobile phone charged.
- Never enter the water, even in an emergency. Reach or throw but don't go

into the water – reach with a broom, mop or towel, or throw a rope (keeping hold of one end), or anything that floats such as a life ring, ball or airtight container.

- *See also* Navigation Notes, page 14, and Stay Safe, page 18.

ENVIRONMENTALLY FRIENDLY BOATING

The Broads area is one of Europe's most important wetlands and conserving this beautiful but fragile environment is one of the responsibilities of the Broads Authority. As part of their work in sustainable tourism (recreation that does no lasting damage to the environment, or to people's enjoyment of it) the Authority actively promotes environmentally friendly boating.

- It is illegal to discharge sewage into the water of the Broads. Anyone doing so may be liable to a fine of up to £2,500. Facilities for pump out and sewage disposal are shown on the relevant map pages.
- Take extra care not to spill diesel into the water when refuelling. Spills of chemicals such as diesel cause harm to wildlife and can kill many water creatures. Spilling diesel or oil is a prosecutable offence.
- If you suspect an oil leak, do not pump out the bilges and release oil into the water. Instead, contact your boatyard immediately.
- If you see a pollution incident of any sort, telephone the Environment Agency on *01733 371811* or the Hotline *0800 80 70 60*
- If you have your own boat, consider electric power. It is clean and convenient and there are charging points around the Broads *(see* Electric Charging Points, page 9). These charging points can also be used to charge on-board batteries: all you need is a cable with an appropriate socket to connect.
- All waste from boats, except sewage, empties straight into the river so that the cleaning products used have a direct impact on the environment. Reduce pollution by using biodegradable washing-up liquid and cleaning products, and try to use detergents containing

no phosphate (also called sodium tripolyphosphate/STPP) or less then 5 per cent. Use only small amounts.

- Do not put cooking oil straight down the sink: absorb oil on to kitchen paper and put the paper in a bin. Oil can cause slicks on the water, causing particular problems for birds.
- Be careful with your rubbish. Discarded litter and fishing tackle can entangle and kill wildlife. Dispose of your rubbish carefully at proper sites. Do not leave bags of rubbish beside the bins, even if they are full – try to hold on to rubbish until you reach the next site.
- Facilities for recycling and waste disposal are often available near moorings or in the local town or village. Details can be obtained from Broads Information Centres.
- Noise pollution should be avoided too. Be sensitive to your neighbours when moored up. Do not leave your engine idling late at night or early in the morning. Also be aware of the volume of your radio or television, particularly when the roof of your boat is down. Causing a noise nuisance could result in a fine of up to £1,000.
- If you have a dog with you, please clear up after it. Remember that although dogs are allowed on public rights of way, under close control, many nature reserves do not allow access for dogs.
- Keep an eye out for the killer shrimp (page 85). Broads users are being urged to **Check, Clean** and **Dry** their boats and fishing equipment, before they enter the water, to help protect the waterways from the invasive killer shrimp. *Dikerogammarus villosus* is an aggressive hunter, feeding on damselflies, small fish, water boatmen and native freshwater shrimp, threatening the Broads eco-system.
- Also be on the lookout for floating pennywort *(see* page 64). It was sold in this country as an ornamental plant for garden ponds, but it has escaped into the wild, where it stops native plants from growing and can cause serious problems for flood control and navigation. Do not

let garden water plants get into the rivers and broads. If you think you have seen floating pennywort in the wild, please contact the Broads Authority or the Environment Agency.

- The Upper Thurne Broads (Hickling, Horsey and Martham) are internationally important for water birds. If you are there during the winter, please avoid the refuge areas (marked by buoys). Large flocks of ducks and geese spend the winter on the open water where they feed and roost and the refuges allow them to stay undisturbed.

- The Green Blue is an environmental awareness initiative supported by the British Marine Federation and the Royal Yachting Association, for those in the marine business and all those who enjoy boating and watersports. Visit *www.thegreenblue.org.uk* or telephone *023 8060 4227* for lots of advice and information.

FUEL

Hire craft usually carry fuel sufficient for the rental period. Many boatyards will include the cost of fuel in the hire price. If you are charged, it will only be for the fuel used, and this will be deducted from your fuel deposit when you return the boat. The *Skipper's Notes* will include more details. Fuel outlets are marked on the map pages.

GOING AGROUND

The Broads is an area of tidal waterways and the tidal effect will be most strongly felt in the Breydon Water area and the lower reaches of the southern rivers. Water levels rise and fall depending upon the state of the tide. It is important to always stay within any channel marking posts. Should you go aground, try reversing gently, or pushing off with the boat hook or quant in the case of yachts. Another method is to get your crew to rock the boat from side to side using the boat hook, or move all crew to the end opposite to that which is aground. If you have any problems, contact your boatyard or telephone Broads Control on *01603 756056*.

LAVATORIES

Hire craft are usually fitted with flushing, sealed unit toilets. They are emptied via a process called 'pump out', which is simple and clean and carried out at boatyards and yacht stations. Pump out facilities are shown on the map pages. Have the toilets pumped out before things become critical. If you are hiring your craft, check the *Skipper's Notes* for more information.

MOORING

Free moorings are available at many locations in the Broads for a maximum stay of 24 hours. These moorings can be used by all boats, and many of them can also be used by anglers. There are also moorings available at public staithes, pubs and boatyards, although there may be a charge to use these.

Mooring up and casting off can be one of the most difficult parts of handling a boat, but with preparation and a little practice you will soon be confident. Plan ahead – make sure that your ropes are ready and that your crew knows what to do. The fittest adult (not a child) should always step (not jump!) ashore and should wear a life-jacket.

- If the mooring is staffed, please follow all directions given by the rangers.

- Always approach a mooring against the tide, with a careful hand on the throttle. You will be able to to hold the boat stationary heading into the tide and approach the mooring sideways under control.

- Always drop your mud weight when moored, especially if mooring stern on (the back of the boat), when the mud weight will stop the bow (the front) swinging around.

- Allow slack in mooring ropes to allow for rises and falls in the water level as the tides rise and fall – check your mooring ropes regularly.

- Do not trail mooring ropes across footpaths and never run alongside moorings, to avoid tripping on ropes or posts.

Sailing regatta near Horning

REGATTAS

Regattas, organised by sailing, power boat and rowing clubs, are very much part of the boating heritage of the Broads. They can be great fun for spectators as well as the participants – bridges are often a good vantage point. Regular events take place each year and details are available from the Broads Information Centres and the Norfolk and Suffolk Boating Association (*www.thegreenbook.org.uk*). If you find yourself on the water during a regatta:

- Keep close to the right hand bank.
- Sailing boats have right of way. Slow down and try to pass behind them.
- Make your course clear – do not weave about.
- Watch for any indications by the crew as to when they would like you to pass, but do not put yourself or others in danger.
- In some areas particular channels may be provided for your safe passage. In these cases stay within the channel. During powerboat racing, do not enter or leave via the body of the broad where the event is taking place.
- Listen carefully to any advice, and follow any guidance from navigation rangers or safety patrol boats.

SLIPWAYS
See Getting Onto the Water, page 6.

SPEED LIMITS
There are speed limits of 3, 4, 5 or 6 mph in force throughout the Broads waterways. The limits are in place to reduce erosion of the river banks, prevent disturbance to water-level nesting birds, and protect people on moored boats. They are clearly signed on the riverbanks and are enforced by the navigation rangers. There is no need to go any faster – the faster you go, the bigger a wave (wash) the boat creates: if your wash is breaking against the bank, causing large waves or throwing moored boats around, slow down. Even if you are under the speed limit, you may still be fined if you are creating excess wash, so check it regularly, especially if you are on a day boat or just getting used to the speed of your boat at the start of a holiday. Slow down also when passing engineering works and anglers, when there is a lot of floating rubbish on the water (try to drift over obvious obstructions in neutral), when approaching blind corners, bridges and junctions. Remember that if your boat is moving in the same direction as the tide, your speed will be faster than indicated.

TIDE TABLES
Tide tables are available from Broads Authority Information Centres and *www.broads-authority.gov.uk*. Local newspapers also publish tide times and the BBC website lists them, at *www.bbc.co.uk/weather/coast*.

TOLLS AND REGISTRATION
See Getting onto the Water, page 6.

WATER
Hire boats will have a full tank of water for drinking and washing. You should top up your water regularly. Water points are indicated on the map pages. If you are hiring a boat, check the *Skipper's Notes* for more information.

WATER SKIING
Water skiing has been a regular Broads activity since 1951. Today there are 10 allocated ski zones on the rivers Waveney and Yare, together with a further zone on Breydon Water. Water skiing may only take place at certain times and all skiers must be members of the Eastern Rivers Water Ski Club and British Water Ski. More information, including the times water skiing is permitted, is available from the Easter Rivers Water Ski club website at *www.erwsc.co.uk*.

- Boat owners must obtain a skiing permit from the Broads Authority.
- All boat drivers must have passed the Sports Boat Drivers Award.
- All boats must have British Water Ski approved public liability insurance.
- Each of the water skiing zones on the Broads is clearly sign-posted. If you cruise through one of the water ski areas you must proceed cautiously as there may be skiers in the water.
- Keep to the right hand side of the river wherever possible.
- Keep a constant speed and course. Stop only to avoid collision or a skier in the water. Ski boats are fast and manoeuvrable and will keep out of your way.
- A yellow flag will be flown by all ski boats when skiing is underway. On seeing the flag, slow down, give the ski boat a wide berth and keep an extra look out for skiers in the water.

WEIL'S DISEASE
See Stay Safe, page 19.

The Broads is generally a safe and trouble-free environment for boating, which is why it is so popular with all boaters, from the experienced to those hiring a boat for the first time. This chapter highlights issues you need to be aware of in advance of your boat trip and provides you with information to help you navigate the Broads waters safely and enjoyably.

ACCIDENTS

If someone is injured or there is serious damage to your boat, or to someone else's, you must stop as soon as is practicable. Call 999 and ask for the coastguard.

- You must inform Broads Control of the incident *(01603 756056)* and give the name and address of the boat owner, and the boat registration number.
- You must also give this information to anyone else who has good reason to request it.
- Hire boaters must also inform their hire centre and there will be instructions on what to do in the *Skipper's Guide.*
- If you have an accident where property is damaged but no one is injured, you must stop your boat and give your name and address, that of the boat owner and the boat registration number, to anyone who has good reason to need it.
- You should take all reasonable steps to find out who the damaged property or boat belongs to, let them know in writing what has happened and give your name and address.
- Report incidents to Broads Control either by telephone *01603 756056*, email *broads.control@broads-authority.gov.uk* via the Broads Authority web site.
- You may be liable to a fine of up to £1,000 if you do not follow these procedures.

BRIDGES

Bridges can be fixed or moveable. Bridge heights shown on the maps are for central clearance at high water on a normal tide. River levels vary considerably, depending upon weather conditions and the tide, and can affect the figures given.

- There is a gauge board on either side of the approach to most bridges, which will give you the current clearance available. Check this carefully to ensure that you have clearance. *See also* page 34.
- The air draft is the height of your boat from the waterline to the highest part of the boat (shown on a plate in the cockpit of hire boats).
- Think ahead when approaching all bridges. Lower the canopy and/or windscreen. Get everyone off the deck. Ensure that all hands and heads are in board in plenty of time before the bridge.
- Never race for a bridge or try to hurry through. Consider moored boats and monitor your boat wash. Keep to the speed limits.
- Watch for other boats coming through. Generally the boat travelling with the current has right of way.
- Don't raise your head until you are well clear of the bridge and **never** try to fend off using hands or feet.
- Yachts will need to lower their masts at all bridges except Reedham, Somerleyton and Trowse swing bridges and the lifting bridges on Breydon Water, and Novi Sad and Carrow Road bridges in Norwich.
- At Potter Heigham hire boats must use the bridge pilot from Phoenix Fleet boatyard to take you through, available *08.30-18.00*, depending on tide and weather conditions. Telephone *01692 670460.*
- At Wroxham there is an optional bridge pilot available to help you. Some hire boatyards insist that their customers use the service – check with the boatyard or look in the *Skipper's Manual.* The service is available *09.00-17.00.* Telephone *07775 297638.*
- If you have any problems, telephone Broads Control on *01603 756056.* The

tidal range is such that passage in one direction does not guarantee a return passage at all times. Check with pilots before proceeding.

Moveable bridges

- At lift and swing bridges, a single red flag indicates the bridge is working and in service; two red flags indicate that the bridge is not working and not in service.
- Bridges will only open for craft clearly unable to pass under (i.e. if you need to lower a canopy or windscreen, you must do so).
- The signal requiring the bridge to open is three prolonged blasts on the horn or whistle.
- Most bridges monitor *VHF channel 12*. The radio will not be answered during emergency matters relating to the rail network.
- The bridge operator will update electronic signage on the bridge to reflect waiting time before the bridge opens.

GREAT YARMOUTH AND BREYDON WATER

You will have to pass through Great Yarmouth and across Breydon Water if you want to cruise between the northern rivers (Bure, Ant and Thurne) and the southern rivers (Yare, Chet and Waveney). This requires careful thought and forward planning.

Great Yarmouth

(*see* Breydon Bridge inset, page 68)

- You must time your arrival in Great Yarmouth to coincide with slack low water or just afterwards. Slack low water is around 1 hour after low water at Great Yarmouth Yacht Station. Check a tide table to find out when this is. At slack low water the current is weaker, so it is easier to moor, and there is more room under the bridges. At high water you will not be able to get under the bridges, and there is nowhere safe to moor to wait for the tide to drop on the Breydon Water side.

- It takes around $2\frac{1}{4}$ hours to travel from Acle to Great Yarmouth, and about 2 hours from Reedham or St Olaves. *See* page 35 for journey times.
- Check the map and follow the directions. The water is shallow outside the posted channel so it is important to keep within the posts.
- You may wait free of charge at Great Yarmouth Yacht Station while the tide drops to allow safe passage under the bridges.
- Always approach the moorings against the tide.
- It may be difficult to turn in the narrow river, so turn well upstream or down, depending on the tide, giving yourself plenty of time.
- If the river is busy, be prepared to go down through the bridges and turn where there is more room.
- You must not proceed downstream if three vertical red lights are on the Yarmouth/Acle Road Bridge.

Breydon Water

(*see* South Breydon Water inset, page 69)

- The Broads Authority operate a ranger patrol in the Breydon Water area.
- In high winds and at high tide, Breydon Water can be rough. Crossing at the right time, at low water, should avoid this problem.
- Everyone should wear a life-jacket when crossing Breydon Water.
- Do not navigate Breydon Water (or anywhere else) in fog.
- The Broads Authority have free 24 hour moorings between the Berney Arms pub and the wind pump (mill). Use them to wait for favourable tides to cross Breydon Water.
- For advice on whether or not to cross, contact your boatyard or telephone Broads Control on *01603 756056*.

INCIDENT REPORTING

All incidents should be reported to Broads Control. *See* Accidents page 14 and Police page 19.

YACHT STATIONS

The Broads Authority run yacht stations at Norwich and Great Yarmouth offering a full range of facilities. They are staffed *daily 08.00-20.00 from Sat before Easter to first week Nov*. There is also a quay attendant at Reedham Quay *daily 09.00-18.00* for the same period. *(Norwich 01603 612980 Great Yarmouth 01493 842794 www. broads-authority.gov.uk/boating/facilities/ yacht-stations).*

NAVIGATION ADVICE

Ask any ranger, or telephone Broads Control on *01603 756056*. The Broads Authority publish *Waterways Code* leaflets covering such subjects as safety and mooring. The leaflets are available from the Authority and their Information Centres, and can also be downloaded from *www.broads-authority.gov. uk/boating/navigating-the-broads.*

NOTICE TO MARINERS

A Notice to Mariners is required whenever any work is undertaken that may significantly affect the navigation, such as river and bridge closures, bridge opening times and special events. The Broads Authority publish the Notices on their website.

RULES OF THE ROAD

- Keep your boat close to the right hand bank.
- Sailing boats have right of way over motor boats. Slow down and try to pass behind them.
- Make your course clear – do not weave about or try to stop suddenly.
- Watch for any indications by other crews as to when they would like you to pass, but do not put yourself or others in danger.
- In some areas particular channels may be provided for your safe passage. In these cases, stay within the channel. During powerboat racing, do not enter or leave via the body of the broad where the racing is taking place.
- Listen carefully to, and take any guidance from navigation rangers or safety patrol boats.

- Keep clear of commercial traffic and watch for any instructions from their crew.
- Keep clear of craft under tow.
- Do not exceed the speed limits.
- Navigation lights are required after dark. (Generally, hire boats may not travel after dark.)
- On the River Yare you may meet coasters travelling between Cantley and Great Yarmouth. They will be escorted by Broads Authority rangers and it is important that you follow their directions.
- You must not fish from a motor or sailing boat which is underway.

SAFE NAVIGATING

- BAM Nuttall contractors are working on flood defences throughout the Broads, which necessitates moving heavy plant and equipment around the waterways. Take note of warning signs and keep clear of the machinery.
- On the western (railway) side of Haddiscoe Cut (page 59), avoid the gabion wire baskets, containing flints. They are there to help build up the flood banks. Stay within the marked posts. Take care when mooring in this area after works have been completed, until the new banks are established.

- A chain-operated ferry operates at Reedham (page 59). Particular care must be taken when it is in operation. Wait until the ferry has docked before passing, to avoid catching the chains with your propeller, and be ready to obey any instruction from the ferry operator.

URGENT BOATING INFORMATION

It is important that all skippers keep up to date with the latest available boating information available from the Broads Authority website. *www.broads-authority. gov.uk/boating/navigating-the-broads/ urgent-boating-information.*

Look out for bigger boats on some of the wider broads.

Boating is a safe pastime. However, it makes sense to take some simple safety precautions. The following notes offer advice to keep you safe during your time on the Broads.

COOKING OUTDOORS

- Do not use barbecues on your boat.
- Keep them away from fuel.
- Do not place them on anything that will burn.
- Do not put them where people will be walking.
- Do not return a smouldering or cooling barbeque to your boat. It will continue to give off deadly carbon monoxide gas until it is completely cold.
- Dispose of them carefully in a bin or skip only when completely cold.

DOGS

Dogs tend to fall overboard quite regularly and are just as susceptible to cold and other water hazards. Keep them safe too. You can buy life-jackets for them as well! Remember that you should never enter the water to rescue a pet – you would be putting your own life at risk.

DON'T JUMP!

The majority of injuries occur through jumping on or off a boat. Step carefully and keep a good handhold.

FIRE SAFETY

Sadly, fire-related accidents and injuries occur on boats every year. Fire can spread quickly on a boat, even on the water, so follow safety precautions and be prepared.

- Be careful with naked flames and never leave the boat with the hob or oven lit. Turn things off until you come back to the boat.
- Familiarise yourself and your crew with the locations and operation of the fire extinguishers. If you are hiring a boat, this should be covered in the boatyard handover and in the *Skipper's Manual*.
- Never block ventilation grills. Boats are enclosed spaces and levels of carbon monoxide can build up from faulty appliances or just from using the cooker.
- If you own your own craft, consider fitting alarms and detectors to help keep you and your crew safe.

- Extinguish all naked flames before refuelling. Turn off the engine and cooker before handling any fuel. Never smoke when refuelling or changing a gas cylinder.
- If in doubt, do not fight a fire yourself. Get out, stay out and wait for the emergency services.
- Visit *www.gov.uk/government/publications/ fire-safety-on-boats* or *www.broads-authority. gov.uk/boating/navigating-the-broads/safety* and take the advice set out in the Boat Safety Scheme website *www.boatsafetyscheme.org/ stay-safe/fire-safety-for-boats*

HANDS AND FEET ARE PRECIOUS

Never try to stop your boat or fend off with your hands or feet. Your hands and feet are much more precious than any boat or structure. Always keep hands and feet inside the boat.

KEEP AN EYE ON YOUR CREW

It is important to know where your crew is at all times. It is possible for people, especially children, to fall overboard without anyone noticing. Do not let children sit on the front of the boat, or play at the stern or on the roof unsupervised, especially when the boat is underway.

LIFE-JACKETS

It is advisable to wear a life-jacket on deck at all times, even if you can swim. Children, the less mobile, and the elderly should always wear a life-jacket, even when the boat is moored. The water is very cold at all times of the year, and even strong swimmers can get into trouble quickly.

MIND YOUR HEAD

Take great care when going through bridges. Make sure that everyone is inside the boat and off the deck, and that all heads and hands are inboard in plenty of time before the bridge. Do not raise your head until you are well past the bridge.

NO SWIMMING

Never swim in the Broads. The water may look inviting, but it is a natural, wild place and always cold, no matter what the time of year or temperature. The cold shock of entering

the water can kill. With your head just above water, you are nearly invisible to boaters. There are lots of hazards underwater such as weed, obstacles, fast currents and the naturally occurring, but poisonous blue-green algae. Areas particularly susceptible to blue-green algae include Barton, Ranworth, South Walsham, Thurne and Whitlingham. *See also* information on Weil's Disease below.

POLICE
The Broads has its own dedicated police officers – the Broads Beat. For non-urgent matters, telephone *101* and ask for the Broads Beat. In any emergency, always telephone *999*.

CARBON MONOXIDE
Carbon Monoxide can kill or make you and your crew seriously ill. When carbon-based, appliance and engine fuels, such as gas, LPG, coal, wood, paraffin, oil, petrol and diesel don't burn completely, CO is produced. Ten simple tips for keeping you and your crew safe are available from *www.boatsafetyscheme. org/stay-safe/carbon-monoxide-(co)/*

REVERSING
Never approach anyone in the water stern (the back of the boat) first. The propeller is located at the stern and will seriously injure anyone in the water.

SPEED AND WASH
See Boating Need to Know, page 12.

STEADY WITH THE DRINK
Relaxing with an alcoholic drink is a pleasant part of a holiday for many people. But, it is essential to keep your wits about you while on the water. It is recommended that the helmsman does not drink until the boat is moored for the night. You can be fined for navigating while not being in proper control of your boat – either through drinking or drug use. Getting on and off the boat, and moving around the deck, during the day and more particularly at night, can be hazardous when you have had a few drinks – you are more likely to fall in, and your chances of survival are reduced.

REFUELLING
- Always switch off your engine and clean up any spillage.
- Do not refuel a boat while underway.
- Fill petrol cans away from the boat – do not refuel the motor directly.
- Petrol must be stored in a low risk position, in compliance with current regulations (available from the Broads Authority).
- Extinguish all naked lights (including pilot lights on fridges, etc) during refuelling.
- Hot surfaces can present a hazard.
- Hire boaters should refer to their *Skipper's Manual* for instructions.

SAFETY ON AND OFF THE WATER
Be very careful alongside water, not just when you are on a boat.
- It is advisable to wear a life-jacket when boarding a boat and getting ashore. Children, weak swimmers, the less mobile and the elderly should wear a life-jacket anywhere near the water's edge.
- Wear suitable clothing and sensible shoes. Check out the weather forecast so that you are prepared.
- Take a torch if you will be returning to your boat after dark.
- When you go ashore, take careful note of your surroundings and any possible hazards. Plan a safe route back to your boat.
- Consider always returning to your boat with a companion, especially if returning late at night.

WEIL'S DISEASE
Weil's disease is a potentially serious, and even fatal condition, which can be contracted from rivers and other water sources, through cuts and scratches. Always wash your hands after contact with the water. If you fall in, wash yourself thoroughly, or shower, and wash your wet clothes before wearing them again. Clean cuts and scratches with an antiseptic and protect them with a plaster. The infection may seem like flu in the early stages and can occur two-four weeks after exposure. If you experience any flu-like symptoms after contact with the water, get medical advice immediately and mention the possibility of Weil's disease – not all medical practitioners will immediately consider it. More information is available from *www.leptospirosis.org.*

■ OTHER ACTIVITIES

Although boating is one of the best ways to enjoy the Broads, there are plenty of opportunities for other activities throughout the area.

ACCESS FOR ALL

Access for everyone is increasing throughout the Broads all the time, from wheelchair accessible boats (for short trips and holidays), to facilities to help people with visual or hearing impairments. For details of wheelchair-friendly hire available, *see* Where to Hire, page 70.

Boardwalks, suitable for wheelchairs and pushchairs, allow everyone to visit the mysterious and swampy woodlands around many of the broads. A list of accessible boardwalks can be found in the Walking section, *see* page 22. For anglers, details of wheelchair accessible fishing platforms may be found under Angling, below. Cycles are available for hire *(see* Cycling, below).

In the chapter on Places to Visit *(see* page 86), we have tried, as far as possible, to note where there is wheelchair access and disabled toilet facilities, and for the nature reserves, to give an indication of accessibility.

The Broads Authority, Broads Information Centres (all have wheelchair access and induction loop systems, although access is limited at Toad Hole Cottage) and Tourist Information Centres can provide more help.

The Broads Authority website contains much information on access, including a list of accessible toilets. The Authority's annual visitor magazine, *Broadcaster*, is available in a large print version, on CD and online at *www.visitthebroads.co.uk/large-print-broadcaster-2017*. Contact the Broads Authority or their Information Centres for more details.

For other contacts, *see* Where to Get More Information, page 24.

ANGLING

The Broads is one of the country's best-known fishing areas, supporting a diversity of species, such as bream, eel, perch, pike, roach, rudd and tench. The coarse fishing season runs from *mid-June to mid-March*. You will need a current Environment Agency licence, available from post offices or online at *www.gov.uk/fishing-licences/buy-a-fishing-licence*. Regular fishing matches take place throughout the area. Some local anglers offer tuition days. Contact the Broads Authority for details or take a look through *Angle on the Broads (see* below).

There are many places to fish from the bank or hire a day boat *(see* Where to Hire, page 70). Fishing platforms suitable for wheelchair users can be found at Rollesby Bridge (page 45), Filby Broad (pages 45-46), the mouth of Upton Dyke (page 44),

An angler fishing from the bank.

Cyclists on Ludham Bridge.

Worlingham Staithe (page 65), Potter Heigham (on the south bank, page 45) and at Martham Pits (page 45; Martham and District Angling Club; *01493 748358; www. marthamanddistrictac.weebly.com*).

The Broads waterways have been strongly associated with pike fishing for many years, and the thought of catching a specimen pike is often a lure for holiday anglers. Pike fossils found in Norfolk date from more than half-a-million years ago and the fish has been hunted in the Broads over hundreds of years, for food and, more recently, for sport. *Angle on the Broads* includes detailed advice on how to catch a pike.

- Never discard fishing tackle, especially baited hooks.
- It is an offence to leave a baited rod unattended. As well as the danger from passing boats, it is potentially hazardous to water birds and fish.
- Watch out for birds swimming into your line. Swans can reach bait deep below the water's surface and other birds will dive for food – wind in your tackle if you think that birds might be at risk.
- Try to ensure that you are visible to approaching boats and acknowledge a boat helm's efforts to keep out of your way.
- If you are fishing from a Broads Authority free mooring, you must give way to boats wishing to moor. Please note that not all

moorings have permission to fish, please see local signage.

- Fish should be returned to the water quickly and gently after weighing (if this is necessary) or after being retained in a keep net. Only use a keep net where necessary and retain fish for the shortest possible time.
- Do not fish from a moving boat. Always wear a life-jacket when fishing from any craft.
- *Angle on the Broads* is a guide published for anglers, containing comprehensive information on fishing on the Broads, including locations for free bank fishing, and details of fishing boat hire and fishing tackle shops. It is available from Broads Information Centres or from the Broads Authority website.

CYCLING

It is fun to explore the Broads by bike, whether you want an easy, family-friendly short route, or something longer and more demanding. There are miles of quiet country lanes, a great choice of bike trails and several Sustrans traffic-free routes through the area.

There is a network of cycle hire centres (*see* Where to Hire, page 70) from where bikes can be hired by the day or half-day, and free cycle route maps are available. Some centres have tandems.

The Bike Hire Association has created nine circular rides ranging from between 9 km (5.5 miles) to almost 37 km (23 miles) which explore the northern Broads area, and include links to off-road routes and a boundary route of 93 km (58 miles). These routes pass interesting places to visit and refreshment stops. You'll enjoy wonderful views of the surrounding countryside and the lakes and rivers.

Route 5 takes in the Norfolk coast between Somerton and Sea Palling (page 40), offering opportunities to explore the beaches.

There is also a Broadland Churches Trail, a circular route of 56 km (35 miles), with shorter options, that takes in 16 beautiful Broadland churches from Hoveton (page 42) to Horning (page 43), via Wroxham, Ranworth, South Walsham and Acle.

The South Trinity Broads Benefice Cycle Trail, another circular route, comprises 20 km (12.5 miles) of easy cycling (with a shorter option), visiting seven special ancient Broads churches. It starts from Filby (page 46) and continues on through Thrigby, Mautby, Runham, Stokesby, Billockby and Fleggburgh (page 45).

The Bure Valley Path is a 14.5 km (9 mile) scenic railway path, for walkers and cyclists, which runs between Aylsham and Wroxham (page 42).

Details of all these routes are available from the cycle hire centres, the Broads Authority and their Information Centres, or visit *www.thebroadsbybike.org.uk* for routes and maps. Norfolk County Council also offers cycle routes on its countryside website (*www.countrysideaccess.norfolk. gov.uk*), as does Suffolk County Council's countryside website (*www.discoversuffolk. org.uk*), where you will find a wide range of short and long distance cycle routes.

Sustrans National Cycle Routes (NCR) 1 and 13, and Regional Route 30 pass through Norfolk. For details of these, Norwich city cycle routes and free cycling maps, visit *www.sustrans.org.uk* or *www.norwich.gov. uk/cycling*.

The Sustrans routes through Suffolk are NCR 1 and 51, and Regional Routes 30 and 41. Again, visit the Sustrans website for full details of these routes and cycle maps for Lowestoft and Beccles.

WALKING

There are more than 306 km (190 miles) of footpaths throughout the Broads, including nature trails, circular walks and long distance footpaths. Remember that dogs are allowed on public rights of way under close control, but many nature reserves do not allow access for dogs.

Broads Walks comprise a collection of short strolls and longer hikes throughout the area, offering opportunities to enjoy each of the Broads rivers. For example, you could take a 4.5 km (3 mile) circular stroll from Irstead Staithe (page 44), or explore the Beccles Marshes (page 65) along a 6.5 km (4 mile) trail or the new footpath to St Benet's from Ludham Bridge. Leaflets of

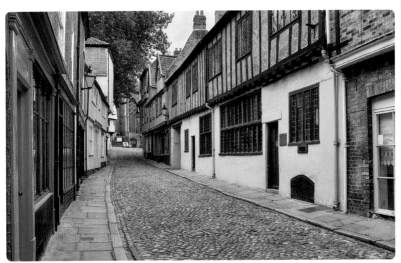

all the walks are available from the Broads Authority and their Information Centres, or visit *www.visitthebroads.co.uk/things-to-do* and download route maps.

There are two series of Broads Walks along public footpaths: the Bure Valley Walks (at Cockshoot, Filby, Oby, Salhouse, Stokesby, Tunstall, Upton and West Caister); and the Waveney Valley Walks (Beccles, Bungay, Burgh Castle, Carlton Marshes, Geldeston, Gillingham and Haddiscoe). Packs containing directions and maps for the walks are available from Broads Authority Information Centres.

Three waymarked long distance footpaths run through the Broads. The Weavers' Way (from Cromer on the north Norfolk coast to Great Yarmouth, page 55) and the Angles Way (from Great Yarmouth to Knettishall Heath Country Park in Breckland, via the Waveney and Little Ouse valleys) are detailed on *www.countrysideaccess.norfolk.gov.uk*, where you can get more information and download route maps. The Wherryman's Way follows the River Yare between Norwich (page 49) and Great Yarmouth (page 55). Visit *www.wherrymansway.net* for lots of useful information, circular walks, access details and descriptions of local heritage highlights

passed en route. The Three Rivers Way is a new circular route for walkers, cyclist and the disabled. Not all sections are complete, there is a section between Horning and Hoveton for cyclists and disabled people using scooters. Plans are underway to complete this part of the route to Ludham and Potter Heigham. There are self-service bike hire points at Hoveton, Horning and Ludham Bridge (page 43)

For more walks in the southern part of the Broads, visit Suffolk County Council's countryside website *www.discoversuffolk.org.uk* which offers routes for a wide range of walks together with details of the several long distance routes through the area.

Boardwalks and easy access paths suitable for wheelchair users can be found at the following Broads locations:

Beccles Marsh Trails (page 65), Chedgrave (page 57), Filby Broad (page 54), Horsey Mere (page 41), Horstead Mill (page 42), Hoveton Riverside Park (page 42), Rockland St Mary (page 57), Salhouse Broad (page 43), Whitlingham Country Park (page 50); and on nature reserves at Barton Broad (page 39), Carlton Marshes (page 66), Cockshoot Broad (page 43), Hickling Broad (page 40), Ranworth Broad (page 43) and Wheatfen (page 57).

The towns and cities of the region can be as charming as the countryside around, like this cobbled street in Norwich.

WHERE TO GET MORE INFORMATION

This chapter contains contact details and web links to help you plan your visit and for when you are in the area. We have included all sorts of different organisations, from the Broads Authority itself to all those others who can provide information and/or services to help make your visit to the area more enjoyable.

The Broads Authority

(see Norwich inset map, page 48)
Yare House, 62-64 Thorpe Road, Norwich, Norfolk NR1 1RY 01603 610734; email broads@broads-authority.gov.uk; www.broads-authority.gov.uk; www.visitthebroads.co.uk

BROADS INFORMATION CENTRES

Knowledgeable staff and the information on offer will help you make the most of your visit to the Broads. Two of the three Centres are open seasonally. During the winter contact the Broads Authority in Norwich or Whitlingham Visitor Centre on *01603 756094.*

Hoveton/Wroxham

Station Road, Hoveton, Norwich, Norfolk NR12 8UR (01603 756097; email hovetontic@broads-authority.gov.uk). Open Easter–Oct, daily 09.00-13.00 and 13.30-17.00.

How Hill

Toad Hole Cottage Museum, How Hill, Ludham, Great Yarmouth, Norfolk NR29 5PG (01603 756096; email toadholetic@broads-authority.gov.uk). Open Easter–Oct, Mon–Fri 10.30-13.00 and 13.30-17.00; Sat–Sun 10.30-17.00. Jun–Sep, daily 09.30-17.00.

Whitlingham Visitor Centre

Whitlingham Lane, near Trowse, Norwich, Norfolk NR14 8TR (01603 756094; email whitlinghamtic@broads-authority. gov.uk). Open Easter–Oct, 10.00-16.00

(closes 17.00 during summer holidays). Nov-Easter most days 11.00-16.00.
The Broads Authority produces an annual visitor magazine, *Broadcaster*, which contains a lot of information on places to stay, things to do and a full events listing. It is available from the Broads Authority and their Information Centres.

TOURIST INFORMATION CENTRES

Open all year.

East of England Tourism

The Grove, Kenninghall Road, Banham, Norfolk NR16 2HE (0333 320 4202; www.visiteastofengland.com). Open Mon-Fri 09.00-17.00.

Great Yarmouth

25 Marine Parade, Great Yarmouth, Norfolk NR30 2EW (01493 846346; email tourism@great-yarmouth.gov.uk; www.great-yarmouth.co.uk/visitor-info).

Lowestoft

East Point Pavilion, Royal Plain, Lowestoft, Suffolk NR33 0AP (01502 533600; email touristinfo@waveney.gov.uk; www.lovelowestoft.co.uk/tourist-information. Open Mon-Sat 10.00-17.00 & Sun 10.00-15.00.

Norwich

The Forum, Millennium Plain, Norwich, Norfolk NR2 1TF (01603 213999; email tic@visitnorwich.co.uk; www. visitnorwich.co.uk Open Mon-Sat 09.30-17.30

MORE WEBSITES FOR VISITORS TO THE BROADS

Discover the Broads, a guide to 12 great days out in the Broads, compiled by people who live there *www.discoverthebroads.com.*
Guide for Norwich, South Norfolk and Broadland *www.visitnorwich.co.uk.*

Norfolk County Council's countryside website *www.countrysideaccess.norfolk.gov.uk.*

Norfolk Tourist Attractions Association *www.norfolktouristattractions.co.uk.*

Norfolk Windmills Trust Union House, Gressenhall, Dereham, Norfolk NR20 4DR (01362 869394; www.norfolkwindmills.co.uk). Contact for details of mill open days.

Suffolk County Council *www.suffolk.gov.uk.*

Suffolk County Council's countryside website *www.discoversuffolk.org.uk.*

OTHER USEFUL CONTACTS

ACCESS FOR ALL
Dial UK (Disability Information Advice Line) *telephone 01302 310123; fax 01302 310404; textphone 01302 310123; email enquiries@dialuk.org.uk; www.dialuk.org.uk. www.scope.org.uk/dial.*

Equality and Human Rights Commission
Telephone: 0808 800 0082; textphone: 0808 800 0084; www.equalityadvisoryservice.com.

RADAR (Royal Association for Disability and Rehabilition) *telephone 020 7250 3222; fax 020 7250 0212; minicom 020 7250 4119; email enquiries@disabilityrightsuk.org; www.accessibletourism.org.*

ANGLING
Martham and District Angling Club *01493 748358*

Norwich and District Pike Club *telephone 01508 578359; email suffolkngood@hotmail.com; www.norwichpike.com*

BOATING
For boatyards, hire centres and booking agencies, *see* Where to Hire, page 70.

Bridge Pilots: Potter Heigham *01692 670460*; Wroxham *07775 297638.*

Boat Safety Scheme *Boat Safety Scheme First Floor North, Station House, 500 Elder Gate, Milton Keynes MK9 1BB telephone 0333 202 1000; www.boatsafetyscheme.org.*

Broads Control, for advice and assistance with navigation on the Broads *01603 756056.*

Canal and River Trust, responsible for maintaining many of the country's canals and inland waterways, *Head Office, First Floor North, Station House, 500 Elder Gate, Milton Keynes MK9 1BB 0303 040 4040; www.canalrivertrust.org.uk.* There are also ten regional offices.

Community boating associations, encouraging more people to access the waterways – for individuals, young people, disabled and other community groups *01922 744637 email info@national-cba. co.uk; www.national-cba.co.uk.*

Environment Agency, manages around 966 km (600 miles) of the country's rivers *03708 506 506 email enquiries@ environment-agency.gov.uk; www.environment-agency.gov.uk.*

Inland Waterways Association, campaigning for the conservation, use, maintenance, restoration and development of Britain's inland waterways *Island House, Moor Road, Chesham, HP5 1WA (01494 783453; www.waterways.org.uk).*

National Association of Boat Owners is dedicated to promoting the interests of private boaters on Britain's waterways *07989 441674; www.nabo.org.uk.* Norfolk and Suffolk Boating Association. The website includes an events programme *www.thegreenbook.org.uk.*

Royal Yachting Association (RYA). The national body for all forms of boating; administers accredited courses for all types of craft.
023 8060 4100; www.rya.org.uk.
The Green Blue, promoting sustainable use of coastal and inland waters *www.thegreenblue.org.uk.*

UK waterways: non-commercial, with more than 2,000 links to canal and waterways related websites *www.canals. com.*

BRIDGE PILOTS *See* Boating, page 25.

CANOEING

Broads Canoe Hire Association, helps you to locate your nearest canoe hire centre *www.canoethebroads.co.uk*

British Canoeing, the UK governing body for the sport *0300 0119500; info@britishcanoeing.org.uk* National Watersports Centre, *Adbolton Lane, Holme Pierrepoint, Nottingham NG12 2LU.*

CYCLING

Cycle routes in the Broads *www.thebroadsbybike.org.uk.*

CTC or Cycling UK, the UK's National Cyclists' Organisation
0844 736 8450/2 www.cyclinguk.org.

For those who like to cycle with a GPS device: lots of routes to share at *www.gps-routes.co.uk.*

Sustrans, the UK's leading sustainable transport charity *70 Cowcross St London EC1M 6EJ 020 7017 2350; www.sustrans.org.uk.*

CHURCH SERVICES

Churches together on the Broads *0790 572149; www.churchestogetheronthebroads.org.uk.*

HEALTH

NHS Direct *0845 46 47; www.nhsdirect.nhs.uk.*

Norfolk and Norwich University Hospital (Norwich) *01603 286286; www.nnuh.nhs.uk.*

James Paget Hospital (Great Yarmouth) *01493 452452; www.jpaget.nhs.uk.*

NATIONAL PARKS

There are 15 members of the National Parks family, including the Broads *029 2049 9966; www.nationalparks. gov.uk. .*

NON-NATIVE SPECIES

The GB Non-Native Species Secretariat. Detailed information and recognition guides *www.nonnativespecies.org.*

POLICE

Telephone *999* in emergencies. The Broads also has its own dedicated police officers. For non-urgent matters, telephone *101* and ask for the Broads Beat.

POLLUTION

For any pollution incident, telephone Broads Control on *01603 756056* (during the day) or the Environment Agency on *01733 371811*. For serious pollution incidents outside office hours, contact the coastguard on *999*.

RADIO CONTROL

See Boating Need to Know, page 9.

TRAVEL

The First number 12 bus offers a service *(Mon–Sat)* from Norwich, taking in a picturesque route through Rackheath, Hoveton, Horning, Ludham and Catfield to Stalham *08456 020 121* or contact Traveline *(see* below).

The Acle area Flexibus serves many Broads villages. It is operated by OURBUS as a demand responsive service – book in advance *01493 752223*. They also operate a limited number of timetabled services.

From Norwich the Bittern railway line *(www.bitternline.com)* goes north through Wroxham; the Wherry line *(www.wherry lines.org.uk)* goes east to Great Yarmouth and Lowestoft. On local services, in Norfolk and Suffolk, cycles are carried free of charge on a first come first served basis. There are four cycle spaces per train. On main line, inter-city services, cycles must be booked in advance by telephoning *0845 600 7245* and selecting option 8. Restrictions apply during weekdays.

Greater Anglia Norwich Railway Station, *Station Approach, Norwich, Norfolk NR1 1EF* for rail travel throughout the region *0845 600 7245* (option 2 for tickets);

Greater Anglia for rail travel throughout the region *0845 600 7245*; *www.greateranglia.co.uk.*

National Rail Enquiries, for information and booking *03457 484950*; *www.nationalrail.co.uk.*

Traveline for public transport information in south and east England *0871 200 2233*; *www.travelineeastanglia.org.uk.*

WALKING

The Long Distance Walkers Association *Bellevue, Princes Street, Ulverston, Cumbria LA12 7NB* promotes walking, especially using long distance paths, email *membership@lwda.org.uk; www.ldwa.org.uk.*

The Ramblers Association, Camelford House, 87-90 Albert Embankment, London, SE1 7TW. The association campaigns for, and encourages, walkers *020 7339 8500; www.ramblers.org.uk.*

The Wherryman's Way, a long distance footpath *www.wherrymansway.net.*

Walking in Norfolk *www.walkinginnorfolk.co.uk.*

Walking in Suffolk *www.walkinginsuffolk.co.uk.*

WATER SKIING

British Water Ski, the national governing body for British water skiing and wakeboarding *01932 560007; www.bwsw.org.uk.*

Easter Rivers Water Ski Club, for water skiing on the Broads *www.erwsc.co.uk.*

WEATHER FORECAST

For the Met Office weather forecast for Norfolk, Suffolk and Cambridgeshire *telephone 0370 900 0100 or 01392 885680; www.metoffice.gov.uk.*

Weather forecasts and tide tables are available from the BBC *www.bbc.co.uk/weather/coast.*

WEIL'S DISEASE

Leptospirosis Information Centre, for information and advice *www.leptospirosis.org.*

WILDLIFE RESCUE

RSPCA *0300 123 4999; www.rspca.org.uk.*

■ EATING OUT

Listed below is a selection of places to eat and drink, many of which have been featured in the Broads Authority *Eating Out Guide*, chosen because they showcase local food and excellence. Other choices are CAMRA recommendations, picked for the selection and quality of their real ales and, in many cases, their food.
The Ⓜ symbol indicates mooring nearby.

ACLE (page 53)

❶ Acle Bridge Inn *Acle Bridge, Old Road, Acle, Norfolk NR13 3AS (01493 750288; www.norfolkbroadsinns.co.uk)*. Riverside pub and restaurant. Children, dogs and muddy boots welcome. Ⓜ

❷ ✕ The Kings Head *The Street, Acle, Norwich NR13 3DY (01493 750204; www.aclekingshead.co.uk)*. Warm, family friendly 18th-C pub in heart of village serving real ales and food. Garden and B&B.

BECCLES (page 65)

3 ✕ ♀ Ristorante Piatto *23 Smallgate, Beccles, Suffolk NR34 9AD (01502 711711; www.pizzapiatto.moonfruit.com)*. Fresh pizza and pasta dishes served in a friendly and lively atmosphere. Ⓜ

4 ✕ ♀ Swan House Restaurant *By St Michael's Tower, Beccles, Suffolk NR34 9HE (01502 713474; www.swan-house.com)*. Bar and *à la carte* menu of seasonal dishes. Advance booking recommended. Ⓜ

BRAMERTON (page 50)

5 ✕ ♀ The Water's Edge Bar & Restaurant *Woods End, Bramerton, Norwich NR14 7ED (01508 538005; www.watersedgewoodsend. co.uk)*. 17th-C riverside inn offering modern à la carte and bar menus in an oak-beamed dining room, with views overlooking the River Yare. Ⓜ

BRUNDALL (page 51)

❻ The Yare *Riverside Estate, Station Road, Brundall, Norwich NR13 5PL (01603 713786)*. Very popular in summer, regularly changing guest beers and good value pub food served *Mon-Thu E, Fri-Sun L&E*. Children welcome

BUNGAY (page 63)

❼ The Green Dragon *29 Broad Street, Bungay, Suffolk NR35 1EF (01986 892681)*. A pub with its own microbrewery, a beer garden and camping. Curry night *every Wed*.

BURGH CASTLE (page 60)

❽ The Fisherman's Inn *Burgh Castle Marina, Burgh Castle, Great Yarmouth, Norfolk NR31 9PZ (01493 780729; www. burghcastlemarina.co.uk/the-fishermans-inn)*. Real ales, locally sourced food and stunning riverside views. Children and well-behaved dogs welcome. Ⓜ

BURGH ST PETER (page 66)

❾ The Waveney Inn *Waveney River Centre, Staithe Road, Burgh St Peter, Beccles, Suffolk NR34 0BT (01502 677599; www. waveneyrivercentre.co.uk)*. Lively, focal point of the River Centre, serving food (including takeaways) and real ale. Camping and lodges. Ⓜ

CATFIELD (page 44)

❿ ✕ The Crown Inn *41 The Street, Catfield, Great Yarmouth, Norfolk NR29 5AA (01692 580128; www.catfieldcrown.co.uk)*. 300-year-old traditional village local, dispensing real ales and home-cooked food. Garden and B&B. Ⓜ

COLTISHALL (page 42)

⓫ The King's Head *Wroxham Road, Coltishall, Norfolk NR12 7EA (01603 737426; www.kingsheadcoltishall.co.uk)*. Real ale and excellent restaurant serving food *L&E*. B&B.

⓬ ✕ The Norfolk Restaurant at the Norfolk Mead Hotel *Church Loke, Norwich, Norfolk NR12 7DN (01603 737531; www.norfolkmead.co.uk)*. Former Georgian merchant's house serving appetising meals sourced from fresh local ingredients. B&B. Ⓜ

FILBY (page 54)

13 ✕ ♀ Filby Bridge Restaurant *Main Road, Great Yarmouth, Norfolk NR29 3AA (01493 368142; www.filbybridgerestaurant.com)*. First class food and superb views over Trinity Broads in a family owned restaurant. *Closed Mon.*

GELDESTON (page 64)

⓮ The Locks Inn *Lock's Lane, Geldeston, Beccles, Suffolk NR34 0HS 01508 518414; www. geldestonlocks.co.uk)*. Occupying a remote location, most easily accessed by boat, this hostelry oozes antiquity and dispenses real ales, ciders and perries. Also tasty snacks and traditional pub food. Riverside garden. Ferry from Beccles Lido. Ⓜ

15 **The Wherry Inn** *7 The Street, Geldeston, Beccles NR34 0LB (01508 518371; www. wherryinn.co.uk).* Delightfully restored village pub serving real ales, with secret courtyards and a garden. Also attached tea room *(open Fri-Sun 11.00-16.00).* Good homemade pub food served *daily L&E and Sun 12.00-18.00.*

GREAT YARMOUTH (page 55)
16 **The Barking Smack** *16 Marine Parade, Great Yarmouth, Norfolk NR30 3AH (01493 859752/07754 116172; www.barkingsmack. com).* Majoring on continental and international beers, many of them on draught. Also real ales and cider from much closer to home. Patio and *summer* barbecues. *Closed Nov-March.*

17 **The Mariners Tavern** *69 Howard Street South, Great Yarmouth, Norfolk NR30 1LN (01493 331164).* Serving a large range of real ales, ciders and perries, this traditional town centre hostelry has a family room, real fires and pub games. *Lunchtime* food.

18 **St John's Head** *58 North Quay, Great Yarmouth, Norfolk NR30 1JB (01493 843443; www.stjohnsheadrealalepub.co.uk).* Situated in one of the oldest areas of the town and serving real ales. Traditional pub games, pool and outdoor drinking area.

19 **The White Swan** *1 North Quay, Great Yarmouth, Norfolk NR30 1PU (01493 842027).* Inexpensive, home-cooked food and real ales in a welcoming and friendly riverside pub. M

HICKLING (page 40)
20 **The Pleasure Boat Inn** *Staithe Road, Hickling, Norwich, Norfolk NR12 0YW (01692 598870; www.ThePleasureboat.com).* Attractive waterside pub with attached café *(open 10.00-16.00)* microbrewery and shop selling non-perishables for boaters. Pub *open all year* serving a range of real ales and ciders, including beers from their microbrewery. Food *L&E* weekdays and *all day Sat-Sun.* Large waterside garden. M

21 **The Greyhound Inn** *The Green, Hickling, Norwich. Norfolk NR12 0YA (01692 598306; www.greyhoundinn.com).* Friendly, family-run village pub, serving real ales and good pub food available *daily L&E.* Attractive garden and outside eating area.

HORNING (page 43)
22 **The Ferry Inn** *Ferry Road, Horning, Norwich NR12 8PS (01692 630259; www. horningferry.co.uk).* Range of lagers and beers, food includes a *daily* carvery, child-friendly menu and large waterside terrace in a popular location near to boatyards.

23 **The New Inn** *54 Lower Street, Horning, Norwich NR12 8PF (01692 631223; www. newinn-horning.co.uk).* Cask ales and wines, traditional homemade classic pub food, *summer opening 08.00* for breakfast, waterside terrace with electric boat hook up. M

24 ✕ **Bure River Cottage Restaurant** *27 Lower Street, Horning, Norfolk NR12 8AA (01692 631421; www.burerivercottagerestaurant.co.uk).* Speciality seafood restaurant, serving mainly local fish and home-grown vegetables. M

25 **The Swan Inn** *10 Lower Street, Horning, Norwich NR12 8AA (01692 630316; www. vintageinn.co.uk).* Dating from 1897 in a dominant, late Victorian building, offering a wide range and beer and food options. Waterside terrace. B&B.

HORSEY (page 41)
26 ✕ **Poppylands** *Waxham Road, Horsey, Great Yarmouth NR29 4EQ (01493 393393).* Located a short distance north of Horsey Wind Pump and the village of Horsey. Poppylands is a traditional 1940s café, with many period artefacts, serving a wide range of traditional favourites including Bubble and Squeak, Bangers and Mash and Spam Fritters. Lunches and teas served to the sound of Vera Lynn, Glenn Miller and the Andrews Sisters. *Open weekdays 10.00-1700, Sun* Carvery. Phone to check *Sun opening* and service.

27 **The Nelson Head** *The Street, Horsey, Norfolk NR29 4AD (01493 393378; www. thenelsonhead.com)* Real ales and real cider together with traditional pub fare, in a welcoming local, close to the sea. Dog- and child-friendly. M

HOVETON (page 42)
28 ✕ ⚲ **Wroxham Barns Restaurant Café** *Tunstead Road, Hoveton, Norwich NR12 8QU (01603 783762; www.wroxhambarns.co.uk/ outlet/grab-a-bite-to-eat).* Home cooked dishes and traditional teas with freshly baked scones and cakes.

LESSINGHAM (page 39)
29 **The Star Inn** *School Road, Lessingham, Norfolk NR12 0DN (01692 580510; www.thestarlessingham.co.uk).* Welcoming

village local, serving real ales and cider, together with meals and bar snacks. Large beer garden, camping and B&B. *Closed Mon.*

LODDON (page 58)

30 **The Angel** *15 High Street, Loddon, Norwich NR14 6ET (01508 520763)*. Well-kept town centre pub with three small cosy bars. Real ales and bar snacks, child- and dog-friendly. Customers are welcome to bring food in from local takeaways. Pool room and garden.

31 ✕ **The Swan** *Church Plain, Loddon, Norwich NR14 6LX (01508 528039; www. theloddonswan.co.uk)*. An independent free house serving local ales, wines and award-winning food *Tue-Sat L&E, Sun lunch 12.00-14.45*. Courtyard garden. B&B.

32 ✕ **The Kings Head** *16 Bridge Street, Loddon, Norwich NR14 6EZ (01508 520330; www.loddonkingshead.co.uk)*. Bar, restaurant, beer garden and large screen TV. Good homecooked food served *Wed-Sun L&E*. Wi-Fi.

LOWESTOFT (page 67)

33 **The Mariners Rest** *60-62 Rotterdam Road, Lowestoft, Suffolk NR32 2HA (01502 218077)*. Deriving its name from its proximity to the cemetery, this welcoming local serves real ales and cider. Enclosed garden and traditional pub games.

34 **The Oak Tavern** *73 Crown Street West, Lowestoft, Suffolk NR32 1SQ (01502 537246)*. A lively drinkers pub, popular with all ages, dispensing real ales. Outdoor patio and traditional pub games.

35 **The Stanford Arms** *94 Stanford Street, Lowestoft, Suffolk NR32 2DD (01502 587444; www.stanfordarms.co.uk)*. The Green Jack Brewery tap serving a good selection of their real ales. Also real cider and pizzas available on *Fri* nights. Real fires and pub games.

36 **The Triangle Tavern** *Triangle Market Place, 29 St Peter's Street, Lowestoft, Suffolk NR32 1QA (01502 582711; www. thetriangletavern.co.uk)*. Attracting a range of ages, this is another outlet for Green Jack ales. Also real cider and an outdoor drinking area. Live music on *Thu and Fri* nights.

LUDHAM (page 44)

37 ✕ **Alfresco Tea Rooms** *Norwich Road, Ludham, Great Yarmouth, Norfolk NR29 5QA (01692 678384)*. Set in a Grade II listed,

thatched cottage, this establishment serves leaf teas in china pots, together with home baked scones and cakes. Breakfast, light lunches and teas. M

38 **The Kings Arms** *High Street, Ludham, Great Yarmouth NR29 5QQ (01692 678386; www.kingsarmsludham.co.uk)*. Significantly extended pub in the heart of the village, serving four real ales and food *12.00-21.00* including carvery *Wed and Sun*. Live music *most Fri*. Pool table and sports TV.

LUDHAM BRIDGE (page 44)

39 ✕ **Wayfarers Café** *Ludham Bridge, Great Yarmouth, Norfolk NR29 5NX(01692 630238; www.facebook.com/wayfarerscafe)*. Situated on the picturesque River Ant, serving a wide selection of hot and cold meals and an *all day* breakfast, food *L&E*. M

40 **The Dog** *Johnsons Street, Ludham, Great Yarmouth NR29 5NY (01692 630321; www. thedogpub.co.uk)*. Beautifully renovated pub, *Open daily 12.00*, serving real ales and a wide range of locally sourced, freshly prepared food. Children and dogs welcome. *Regular* live music, garden and camping. Quiz *Sun*.

MARTHAM (pages 45)

41 ✕ **The Kings Arms** *15 The Green, Martham, Great Yarmouth NR29 4PL (01493 749156)*. Friendly pub in the heart of the village overlooking village pond, serving real ales and cider. Home cooked food served *daily 12.00*. Children in restaurant and garden only *after 18.00*.

NEATISHEAD (pages 43)

42 ✕ **The White Horse Inn** *The Street, Neatishead, Norwich NR12 8AD (01692 630828; www.thewhitehorseinnneatishead.com)*. Delightful village pub and restaurant majoring on real ale, craft and bottled beers. Wide range of bar and restaurant food freshly prepared and sourced from local suppliers. Child- and dog-friendly.

NORWICH (pages 48-50)

43 **The Fat Cat & Canary** *101 Thorpe Road, Norwich, Norfolk NR1 1TR (01603 436925; www.fatcatcanary.co.uk)*. 1/3rd mile west of Thorpe Green moorings. This pub serves most of the local Fat Cat Brewery's ales together with brews (including real cider) from further afield. Beer garden. *Sun* roasts *12.00-17.00* M

44 The Compleat Angler *120 Prince of Wales Road, Norwich NR1 1NS (01603 622425; www.greenking-pubs.co.uk/thecompleatangler).* Roomy, traditional pub, serving cask ales and classic British food. Riverside terrace overlooking moorings. M

45 The King's Head *42 Magdalen Street, Norwich, Norfolk NR3 1JE (01603 620468; www.kingsheadnorwich.com).* Friendly, welcoming establishment dispensing real ales from East Anglian breweries, together with real cider. Traditional pub games.

46 ✕ The Old Rectory Hotel *103 Yarmouth Road, Norwich, Norfolk NR7 0HF (01603 700772; www.oldrectorynorwich.com).* Delightful Georgian Country house-style hotel, serving an ever-changing daily menu. B&B. M

47 The Plough *58 St Benedicts Street, Norwich, Norfolk NR2 4AR (01603 661384; www.theploughnorwich.co.uk).* The Grain Brewery tap, close to Norwich Arts Centre, dispensing real ales and their renown sausage pie and *summer* barbecues. Courtyard garden and real fires in *winter*.

48 The Ribs of Beef *24 Wensum Street, Norwich, Norfolk NR3 1HY (01603 619517; www.ribsofbeef.co.uk).* Appetising meals using locally sourced ingredients, together with real ales, cider and foreign beers are the stock in trade of this popular waterside pubs. M

49 Take 5 *17 Tombland, Norwich, Norfolk NR3 1HF (01603 763099).* Set in a Grade II, listed building – in part dating from 15th C – this hostelry dispenses real ales from local breweries and high quality home made food, with a good vegetarian choice. Also real cider, a good selection of bottled beers and organic wines.

50 The Trafford Arms *61 Grove Road, Norwich, Norfolk County NR1 3RL (01603 628466; www.traffordarms.co.uk).* Run by the same licensees for more than 20 years, this welcoming pub serves a wide range of real ale and tasty, homemade food. Pub games and real fires in *winter*.

51 ✕ The Vine *7 Dove Street, Norwich, Norfolk NR2 1DE (01603 627362; www.vinethai.co.uk).* A telling combination of real ales and Thai cuisine, served in this tiny gem of a pub in the heart of the city. Outdoor drinking area and traditional pub games.

52 The White Lion *73 Oak Street, Norwich, Norfolk NR3 3AQ (01603 632333; www.individualpubs.co.uk/whitelion).* CAMRA cider pub of the year – selling a range of over 20 ciders and perries – also dispensing real ales and good value food (with many cider-based recipes). Traditional pub games and real fires in *winter*.

53 The Wig & Pen *6 St Martin-At-Palace Plain, Norwich, Norfolk NR3 1RN (01603 625891; www.thewigandpen.com).* Immediately opposite the Bishop's Place, this friendly 17th-C hostelry dispenses real ales and excellent food *lunchtimes* and *evenings*. Outdoor drinking area and real fires in *winter*.

ORMESBY ST MICHAEL (page 46)
54 ✕ The Boat House *Eels Foot Road, Ormesby St. Michael, Norfolk NR29 3LP (01493 730342; www.theboathouseormesbybroad.co.uk).* On the banks of Ormesby Broad, in 11 acres of grounds, serving superb freshly prepared food *L&E* and a small but ever changing range of ales.

OULTON BROAD (page 67)
55 ✕ Quayside Bar and Restaurant *Broadland Holiday Village, Marsh Road, Oulton Broad, Lowestoft, Suffolk NR33 9JY (01502 500895; www.broadlandvillage.co.uk).* Offering a blend of local ales, snacks and light lunches, a carvery on *Sun lunchtime* and *Wed evenings*. Caravans, lodges and bungalows. M

56 ✕ ♀ Red Herring Restaurant *152 Bridge Road, Oulton Broad, Lowestoft, Suffolk, NR33 9JT (01502 566499; www.redherringwinebar.com).* Restaurant, tapas and wine bar situated in the old port area of Oulton Broad with food available *all day*. Courtyard tables and live music. M

57 ✕ The Wherry Hotel *Bridge Road, Oulton Broad, Lowestoft NR32 3LN (01502 516845; www.wherryhotel.com).* Grand Victorian building overlooking the sea front at the head of Oulton Broad serving real ales, full English breakfast and *all day carvery 12.00-22.00.*

58 The Commodore *15 Commodore Road, Oulton Broad, Lowestoft NR32 3NE (01502 508231; www.moss-co.com).* A modernised traditional building. in an elevated position, with stunning views from the terraced garden over Oulton Broad. Range of real ales, freshly-cooked food using local and seasonal ingredients.

PAKEFIELD (page 67)

59 **The Oddfellows** *6 Nightingale Road, Pakefield, Suffolk NR33 7AU (01502 538415).* A plethora of wood (floors and panelling) cocoon drinkers in this small, cosy pub, serving real ales and excellent food. Outside seating area.

POTTER HEIGHAM (page 45)

60 **Falgate Inn** *Ludham Road, Potter Heigham, Great Yarmouth NR29 5HZ (01692 670003).* 18th-C pub with oak beams and an open fire. Good value pub food served in an extended restaurant area. Booking essential on boat change over days. Garden. B&B.

REEDHAM (page 59)

61 **The Reedham Ferry Inn** *Ferry Road, Norwich NR13 3HA (01493 700429; www.reedhamferry.co.uk).* Fresh food, with an emphasis on local fish, served alongside real ales and the River Yare. Outside seating. Fishing and camping. Showers. M

62 **The Ship Inn** *12 Riverside, Reedham Norwich NR13 3TQ (01493 700287; www.shiphotelnorfolk.co.uk).* Range of real ales and tradition pub food served *daily L&E,* pool table and sports TV. Riverside garden adjacent to the historic railway swing bridge: an excellent place to watch the world go by.

ROCKLAND ST MARY (page 57)

63 **The New Inn** *12 New Inn Hill, Rockland St Mary, Norwich NR14 7HP (01508 538211; www.thenewinnrockland.co.uk).* Standing at the head of Rockland St Mary Staithe, on a short arm off the River Yare, the New Inn is a village pub offering an excellent selection of real ales and good homemade food *L&E.* Garden, children welcome.

ROLLESBY (page 46)

64 **The Waterside Rollesby** *Main Road, Rollesby, Norfolk NR29 5EF (01493 740531; www.thewatersiderollesby.co.uk).* Serving an extensive selection of homemade cakes, teas and light lunches by day, this Broadside restaurant becomes a haven for fine dining at night. Boat hire, including wheelchair accessible.

SHADINGFIELD (page 65)

65 **The Fox** *London Road, Beccles, Suffolk NR34 8DD (01502 575100; www.shadingfieldfox.co.uk).* With its origins in the 16th C, this welcoming hostelry dispenses real ales and excellent food. Patio, small garden, family room and open fires. Live music *Fri.*

SMALLBURGH (page 38)

66 **The Crown Inn** *Smallburgh, Norwich, Norfolk NR12 9AD (01692 536314; www.thecrowninnsmallburgh.co.uk).* This partially thatched, 15th-C coaching inn serves a good range of real ales and appetising food. An open fire, traditional pub games, garden and B&B.

SOMERLEYTON (page 66)

67 **The Dukes Head** *Slugs Lane, Somerleyton, Lowestoft NR32 5QR (01502 730281; www.thedukesheadsomerleyton.co.uk).* Open all day, dispensing a range of Suffolk real ales, together with world beers. Good, varied food, from a fresh, seasonal menu *L&E. Sunday roast 12.00-17.00.* Outside seating. B&B.

SOUTH WALSHAM (page 44)

68 **Fairhaven Woodland and Water Garden Tea Room** *School Road, South Walsham, Norfolk NR13 6DZ (01603 270449; www.fairhavengarden.co.uk).* Family-friendly café, incorporated into a beautiful woodland and water garden, serving homemade pastries, hot food, light lunches and teas. M

69 **Kings Arms Pub Chinese & Thai Restaurant** *1 Panxworth Road, South Walsham, NR13 6DY (01603 270039; home.btconnect.com/broadlandchinese).* Blend of pub and oriental eatery serving old favourites alongside more exotic innovations. Taxi and delivery service. M

STALHAM (page 39)

70 **The Mermaids Slipper** *1 Staithe Road, Stalham, Norwich NR12 (01692 580808/07899 843013; www.the-mermaids-slipper.co.uk).* Excellent food in a beautiful setting – a restaurant for special occasions. *Open evenings Thu-Sat and Sun lunchtimes.* Booking essential.

STOKESBY (page 53)

71 **The Ferry Inn** *Riverfront, The Green, Stokesby, Norfolk NR29 3EX (01493 751096; www.ferryinn.net).* Traditional fare and real ales are served in this riverside pub. Family- and dog-friendly. Garden with picnic tables. M

ST OLAVES PRIORY (page 59)

72 **Priory Restaurant** *St Olaves, Great Yarmouth NR31 9HE (01493 488432; www.prioryfarmrestaurant.co.uk).* Good food with British based menu and bar serving beers and wines.

SURLINGHAM (page 51)

73 **The Ferry House** *1 Ferry Road, Surlingham Norwich NR14 7AR (01508 538659; www.surlinghamferry.co.uk).* Traditional riverside country pub, opened in 1725, serving three regular beers together with a selection of homemade food served *all day*. Breakfast *from 09.00* – booking only. Families and dogs welcome, *winter* fires.

74 ✕ **Coldham Hall Tavern** *Coldham Hall Carnser, Surlingham, Norfolk NR14 7AN (01508 538366; www.coldhamhalltavern.co.uk).* Real ales and meals sourced from local ingredients are the staple of this riverside pub. Garden.

SWANTON ABBOTT (page 38)

75 ✕ **The Jolly Farmers** *North Walsham Road, Swanton Abbott, Norfolk NR10 5DW (01692 538863).* Traditional village local, with a strong leaning towards pub games, serving real ales. Food *Fri only*. Garden, open fire.

THURNE (page 44)

76 **The Lion Inn** *The Street, Thurne, Norfolk NR29 3AP (01692 671806; www. thelionatthurne.com).* Recently refurbished pub, standing at the head of a short inlet, serving a range of 24 beers and ciders, food *L&E*. Garden, dogs and children welcome. Telephone for *winter opening hours*.

TROWSE (page 50)

77 **The White Horse** *The Street, Trowse, Norfolk NR14 8ST (01603 622341; www. whitehorsetrowse.co.uk).* Overlooking the village green (complete with children's playground), this pub serves real ales and home cooked food. Garden, real fires, traditional pub games. Wi-Fi.

UPTON (page 52)

78 **The White Horse** *17 Chapel Road, Upton, Norfolk NR13 6BT (01493 750696; www.whitehorseupton.com).* 100% community owned, this historic Broadlands pub is a short stroll from the idyllic Upton Marshes. Family- and dog-friendly, real ales and appetising, home cooked food. Garden.

WALCOTT (page 39)

79 **The Lighthouse Inn** *Coast Road, Walcott, Norfolk NR12 0PE (01692 650371; www.lighthouseinn.co.uk).* Family-friendly pub with a large garden, serving real ales and excellent homemade food, using fresh local ingredients. Real fires, traditional pub games and camping.

WAYFORD BRIDGE (page 39)

80 ✕ **Wayford Bridge Inn** *Wayford Road, Stalham, Norwich NR12 9LL (01692 582414; www.wayfordbridge.co.uk).* Three-star riverside hotel, bar and restaurant, with parts dating from the 17th C, set amid acres of attractive landscaped gardens.

WINTERTON-ON-SEA (page 46)

81 **The Fisherman's Return** *The Lane, Winterton-on-Sea, Great Yarmouth, Norfolk NR29 4BN (01493 393305; www. fishermansreturn.com).* A hidden gem retaining many of its original 17th-C features. Majoring on food and family-friendly. Real ales and B&B.

WOODBASTWICK (page 43)

82 **The Fur & Feather Inn** *Slad Lane, Woodbastwick, Norfolk NR13 6HQ (01603 720003; www.thefurandfeather.co.uk).* Housed in three old cottages, this welcoming hostelry serves real ales (from the adjoining Woodforde's Brewery) and excellent food. Family room and large garden.

Many riverside pubs and inns have moorings to attract passing boaters

Eating Out

33

Average clearance at high water is given but always check bridge gauge boards. Think ahead when approaching all bridges. Lower the canopy and/or windscreen. Get everyone off the deck. Ensure that all hands and heads are inboard in plenty of time before bridge. *See also* Navigation Notes, page 14.

SPEED LIMIT

Speed limits range from 3 to 6 mph – please comply with them. Look out for the warning signs. *See also* Boating Need to Know, page 13.

CAUTION

Water ski area. Keep a steady course to the right hand side of the channel. *See also* Boating Need to Know, page 13.

Overhead cables.

Yachts must lower their masts at all bridges except Reedham, Somerleyton and Trowse swing bridges, the lifting bridges on Breydon Water, the Novi Sad swing pedestrian bridge in Norwich and the lifting bridge at Carrow Road, Norwich.

There are set times at which Trowse rail bridge opens *(see www.broads-authority.gov. uk)*. The Broads Authority website also has a list of bridge clearance measurements. These are given for Average High Water during the summer. Note that there will be greater clearance at Low Water, especially at Great Yarmouth and in the southern rivers. As well as the state of the tide, river levels can be affected by rainfall and wind conditions. Always exercise caution when approaching any bridge and carefully note the bridge gauge board. *See also* Navigation Notes, page 44.

Rivers Bure, Ant and Thurne — hours

	Ant Mouth	Barton Broad	Coltishall	Great Yarmouth	Hickling Staithe	Horning	Potter Heigham	Stalham	Stracey Arms Mill	Thurne Mouth	Wroxham
Acle	1	2¼	4¾	2¼	2½	2	1¼	3	1	½	3¼
Ant Mouth		1¼	3¾	3½	2½	1	1¼	2	2	½	2¼
Barton Broad			5	4¾	3¾	2¼	2½	¾	3¼	1¾	3½
Coltishall				7¼	6¼	2¾	5	5¾	5¾	4¼	1½
Great Yarmouth					4¾	4¼	3¾	5½	1½	3	5½
Hickling Staithe						3½	1¼	4½	3¼	2	4½
Horning							2¼	3	3	1½	1¼
Potter Heigham								3¼	2¼	¾	3½
Stalham									4	2½	4¼
Stracey Arms Mill										1½	4
Thurne Mouth											2¾
Wroxham											

Rivers Yare, Chet and Waveney — hours

	Beccles	Berney Arms Mill	Brundall	Burgh Castle	Cantley	Geldeston	Great Yarmouth	Loddon	Norwich Yacht Station	Oulton Broad Yacht Station	Oulton Dyke	Reedham	St Olaves
Berney Arms Mill	4												
Brundall	5½	3											
Burgh Castle	3¾	¼	3¼										
Cantley	4¼	1¾	1¼	2									
Geldeston	1	5	6½	4¾	5¼								
Great Yarmouth	4¾	¾	3¾	1	2¾	5¼							
Loddon	4¾	2¼	2¾	2½	1½	5¾	3						
Norwich Yacht Station	7½	5	2	5¼	3¼	8½	5¾	4¾					
Oulton Broad Yacht Station	2¼	2¾	4¼	2½	3	3¼	3½	3½	6¼				
Oulton Dyke	1¾	2¼	3¾	2	2½	2¾	3	3	5¾	½			
Reedham	3¼	1	2	1¼	1	4¼	1¾	1¼	4	2¼	1¾		
St Olaves	2¾	1¼	2¾	1	1¾	3¾	2	2	4¾	1½	1	¾	
Thorpe Green	6¾	4½	1½	4¾	2½	7¾	5¼	4¼	½	5¾	5¼	3½	4¼

Waterways Signs and Journey Times

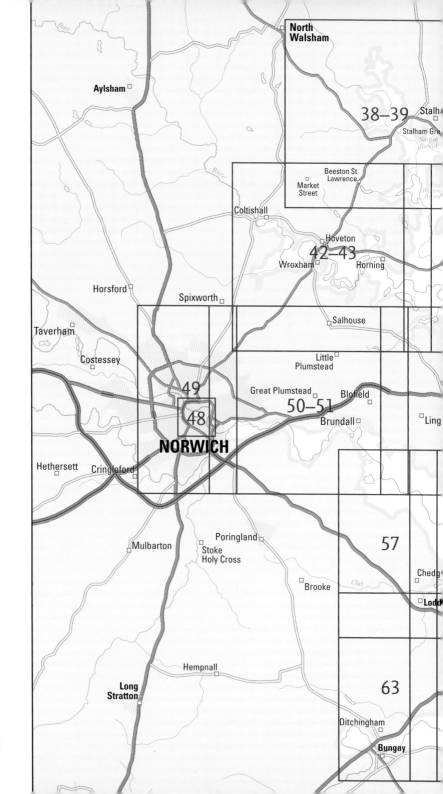

North Walsham

Aylsham

38–39

Stalh

Stalham Gre

Beeston St Lawrence

Market Street

Coltishall

Hoveton

42–43

Wroxham

Horning

Horsford

Spixworth

Salhouse

Taverham

Costessey

Little Plumstead

49

Great Plumstead

Blofield

50–51

Ling

48

Brundall

NORWICH

Hethersett

Cringleford

Mulbarton

Poringland

Stoke Holy Cross

57

Brooke

Chedg

Lodd

Hempnall

63

Long Stratton

Ditchingham

Bungay

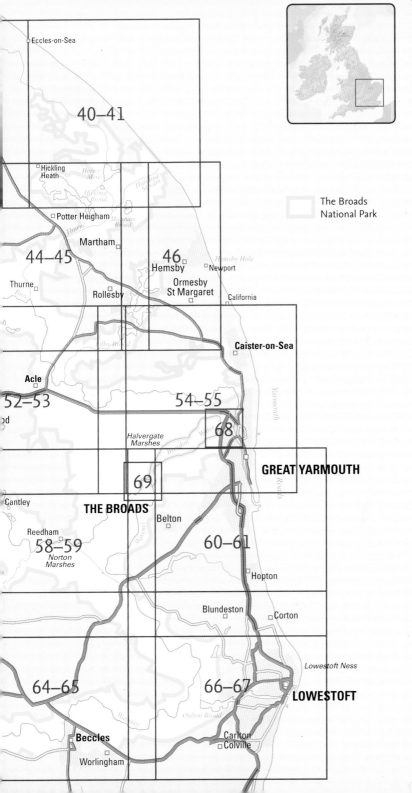

Eccles-on-Sea

40–41

Hickling Heath

Horse Mere

Hickling Broad

Heigham Sound

Potter Heigham

Thurne

Martham Broad

44–45

Martham

46

Hemsby

Hemsby Hole

Newport

Thurne

Rollesby

Ormesby
St Margaret

California

Filby Broad

Caister-on-Sea

Acle

52–53

od

54–55

Yarmouth

68

Halvergate Marshes

Breydon Water

GREAT YARMOUTH

Roads

69

Cantley

THE BROADS

Belton

Reedham

58–59

Norton Marshes

60–61

Hopton

Blundeston

Corton

64–65

Lowestoft Ness

66–67

LOWESTOFT

Oulton Broad

Beccles

Carlton
Colville

Worlingham

☐ The Broads
  National Park

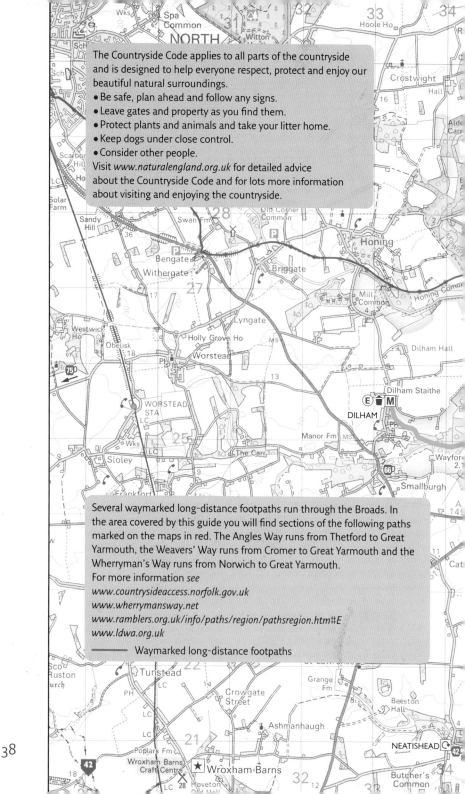

The Countryside Code applies to all parts of the countryside and is designed to help everyone respect, protect and enjoy our beautiful natural surroundings.
- Be safe, plan ahead and follow any signs.
- Leave gates and property as you find them.
- Protect plants and animals and take your litter home.
- Keep dogs under close control.
- Consider other people.

Visit *www.naturalengland.org.uk* for detailed advice about the Countryside Code and for lots more information about visiting and enjoying the countryside.

Several waymarked long-distance footpaths run through the Broads. In the area covered by this guide you will find sections of the following paths marked on the maps in red. The Angles Way runs from Thetford to Great Yarmouth, the Weavers' Way runs from Cromer to Great Yarmouth and the Wherryman's Way runs from Norwich to Great Yarmouth.

For more information *see*
www.countrysideaccess.norfolk.gov.uk
www.wherrymansway.net
www.ramblers.org.uk/info/paths/region/pathsregion.htm#E
www.ldwa.org.uk

—————— Waymarked long-distance footpaths

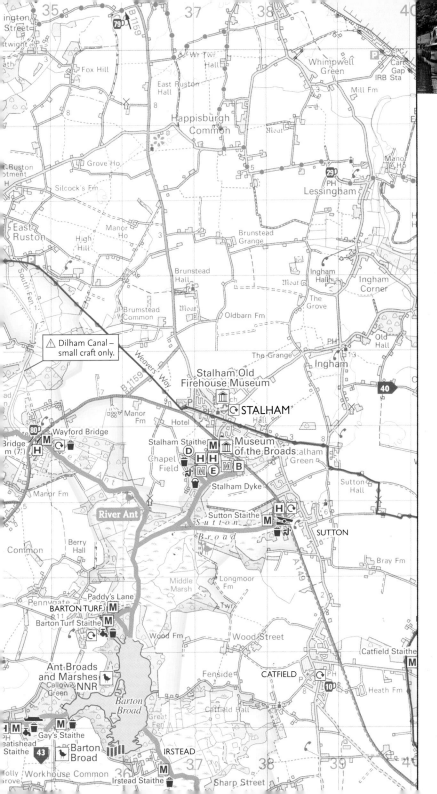

⚠ Dilham Canal – small craft only.

Stalham Old Firehouse Museum

STALHAM

Museum of the Broads

Stalham Staithe

River Ant

Wayford Bridge

Stalham Dyke

Sutton Staithe

SUTTON

Paddy's Lane

BARTON TURF

Barton Turf Staithe

Ant Broads and Marshes NNR

Barton Broad

Gay's Staithe

Barton Broad

IRSTEAD

Irstead Staithe

CATFIELD

Catfield Staithe

Whimpwell Green

Lessingham

Ingham Corner

Ingham

East Ruston Hall

Happisburgh Common

Fox Hill

Grove Ho

Silcock's Fm

East Ruston

Manor Ho

High Hill

Brunstead Grange

Ingham Hall

The Grove

Oldbarn Fm

The Grange

Brunstead Hall

Brunstead Common

Weavers' Way

Manor Fm

Hotel

Chapel Field

Manor Fm

Common

Berry Hall

Middle Marsh

Longmoor Fm

Wood Fm

Wood Street

Fenside

Catfield Hall

Bray Fm

Sutton Hall

Stalham Green

Pennygate

Callow Green

Great Fen

Heath Fm

Sharp Street

39

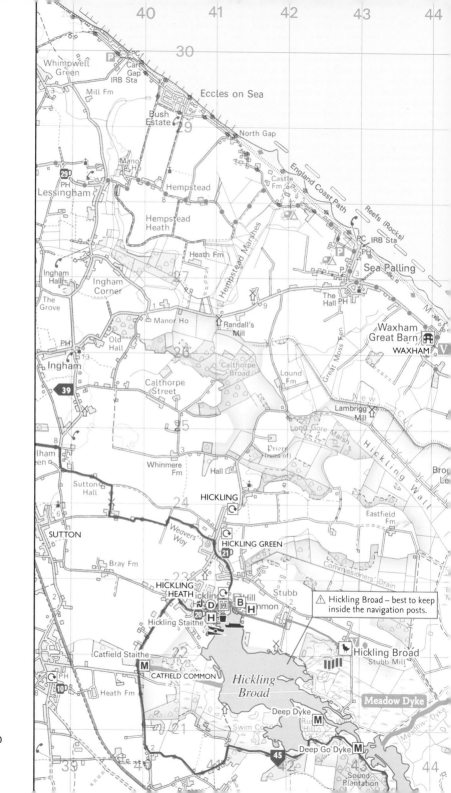

Whimpwell Green
PC
Car Gap
IRB Sta
Mill Fm
Eccles on Sea
Bush Estate
North Gap
Manor
Manor LH
PH
Lessingham
Hempstead
Castle Fm
England Coast Path
Reefs (Rocks)
PC IRB Sta
PH
Sea Palling
Hempstead Heath
Heath Fm
Hempstead Marshes
The Hall PH
P
Ingham Hall
Ingham Corner
Waxham Great Barn
The Grove
PH
Manor Ho
Randall's Mill
WAXHAM
V
Old Hall
Calthorpe Broad
Lound Fm
Great Moss Fen
Ingham
39
Calthorpe Street
Lambrigg Mill
Long Gore Marsh
Hickling Wall
Whinmere Fm
Hall
Priory (ruins of)
Broad Le
Sutton Hall
HICKLING
Eastfield Fm
SUTTON
Weavers' Way
HICKLING GREEN
21
Commissioners' Drain
Bray Fm
Stubb
HICKLING HEATH
Hickling
Hill
mon
B
H
△ Hickling Broad – best to keep inside the navigation posts.
D M
H
20
Hickling Staithe
Catfield Staithe
M
CATFIELD COMMON
Hickling Broad
Stubb Mill
Hickling Broad
PH
10
Heath Fm
Deep Dyke
M
Swim Coo
Meadow Dyke
Deep Go Dyke
M
45
Sound Plantation

Horsey Mere is open to the public from spring to autumn. There is a path from the Mere along the banks of the Waxham New Cut to the remains of Brograve Drainage Mill. Another path leads to a viewpoint over Horsey Mere.

⚠ Waxham New Cut – narrow and difficult to turn.

⚠ CAUTION – overhead cables.

⚠ Beware of weed around edges in summer. Voluntary ban on all craft in winter.

Horsey Wind Pump

Horsey Mere

41

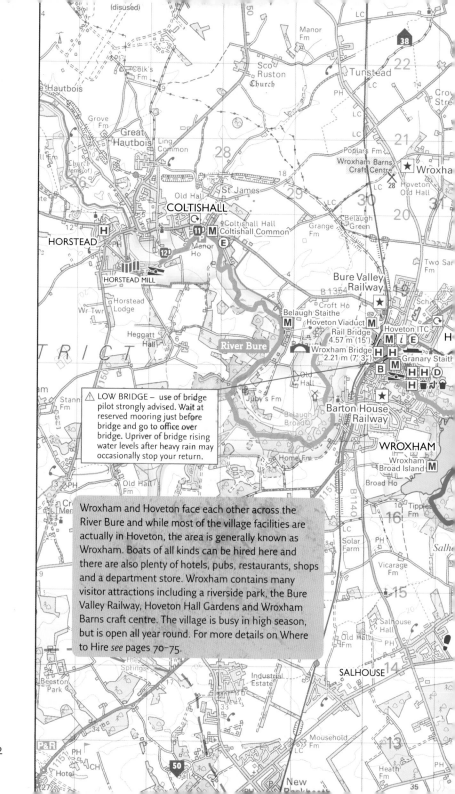

LOW BRIDGE – use of bridge pilot strongly advised. Wait at reserved mooring just before bridge and go to office over bridge. Upriver of bridge rising water levels after heavy rain may occasionally stop your return.

Wroxham and Hoveton face each other across the River Bure and while most of the village facilities are actually in Hoveton, the area is generally known as Wroxham. Boats of all kinds can be hired here and there are also plenty of hotels, pubs, restaurants, shops and a department store. Wroxham contains many visitor attractions including a riverside park, the Bure Valley Railway, Hoveton Hall Gardens and Wroxham Barns craft centre. The village is busy in high season, but is open all year round. For more details on Where to Hire *see* pages 70–75.

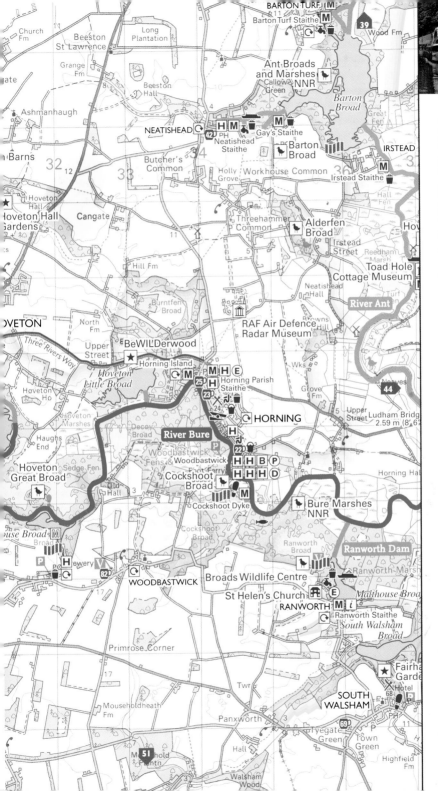

Church Fm

Beeston St Lawrence

Long Plantation

BARTON TURF **M**

Barton Turf Staithe

Wood Fm

39

Grange Fm

Beeston Hall

Ant Broads and Marshes NNR

Callow Green

Barton Broad

Great Fen

Ashmanhaugh

Butcher's Common

H M PH **42** Neatisthead Staithe

NEATISHEAD

Gay's Staithe

M

Barton Broad

IRSTEAD

Barns

32 12

33

34

Holly Grove

Workhouse Common

36

Irstead Staithe **M**

Hoveton Hall Gardens

Cangate

Threehammer Common

11

Alderfen Broad

Irstead Street

Reedham Marsh

Hov

Hill Fm

Toad Hole Cottage Museum

OVETON

North Fm

Burntfen Broad

River Ant

Neatishead Hall

Browns Hill

RAF Air Defence Radar Museum

Wks

44

Three Rivers Way

Upper Street

BeWILDerwood

Horning Island **M**

M H E

Horning Parish Staithe

H

Grove Fm

Upper Street

Ludham Bridge 2.59 m (8' 6")

Hoveton Little Broad

25

23

24

HORNING

Hoveton Ho

Hoveton Marshes

Decoy Broad

H

Haughs End

Woodbastwick Fens

Woodbastwick Foot Ferry

H

P

22

H H B P

H H H D

M

Horning Hall

Hoveton Great Broad

Sedge Fen

Cockshoot Broad

Cockshoot Dyke

Bure Marshes NNR

Old Hall

3

Ranworth Dam

use Broad **M**

Cockshoot Broad

Ranworth Broad

Ranworth Marsh

P

H ewery **V**

82

WOODBASTWICK

Broads Wildlife Centre

St Helen's Church

RANWORTH

Malthouse Broad

E

M *i*

Ranworth Staithe

South Walsham Broad

17

Primrose Corner

17

Fairha Garde

Mouseholdheath Fm

Panxworth

Twr

Hotel

68

P

SOUTH WALSHAM

69

yegate Green

Town Green

11

old antn **51**

Hall

Highfield Fm

Walsham Wood

43

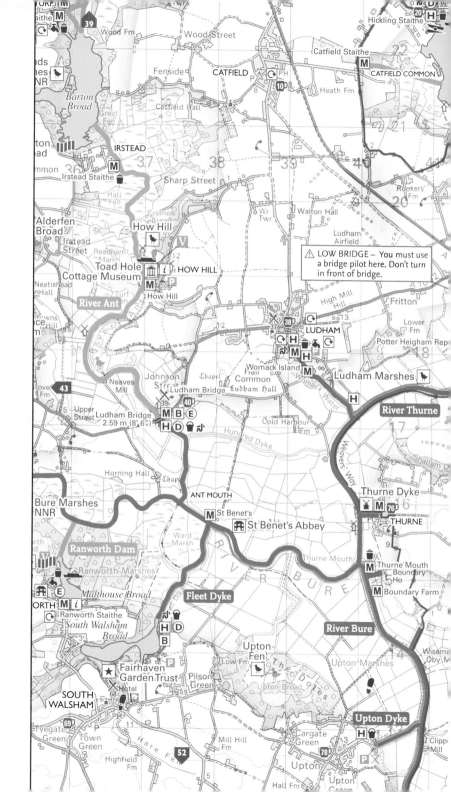

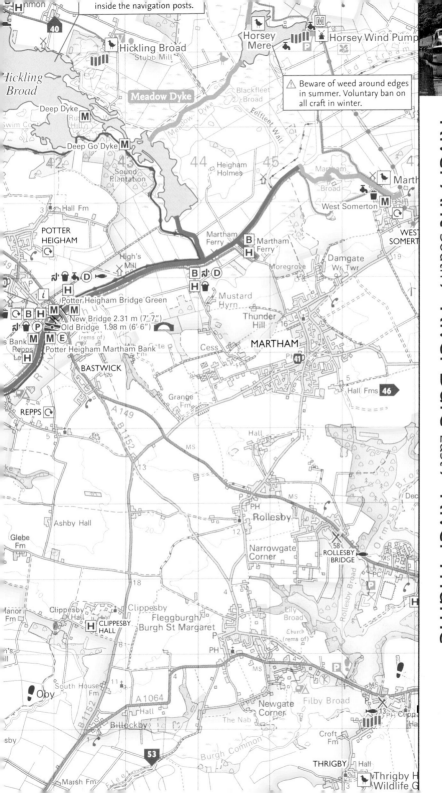

inside the navigation posts.

Horsey Wind Pump

⚠ Beware of weed around edges in summer. Voluntary ban on all craft in winter.

Hickling Broad

Stubb Mill

Hickling Broad

Meadow Dyke

Deep Dyke

Deep Go Dyke

Heigham Holmes

West Somerton

Martham Ferry

Martham Ferry

POTTER HEIGHAM

High's Mill

Hall Fm

Mustard Hyrn

Potter Heigham Bridge Green

New Bridge 2.31 m (7' 7")
Old Bridge 1.98 m (6' 6")

Thunder Hill

Potter Heigham Martham Bank

MARTHAM

BASTWICK

Grange Fm

Hall Fms

REPPS

A149

Cess

Ashby Hall

Hall

Rollesby

Glebe Fm

Narrowgate Corner

ROLLESBY BRIDGE

Clippesby

Clippesby Hall

Fleggburgh/ Burgh St Margaret

CLIPPESBY HALL

Lily Broad

Church (rems of)

Oby

South House Fm

Newgate Corner

Filby Broad

The Nab

Billockby

Croft Fm

Burgh Common

THRIGBY

Thrigby H Wildlife G

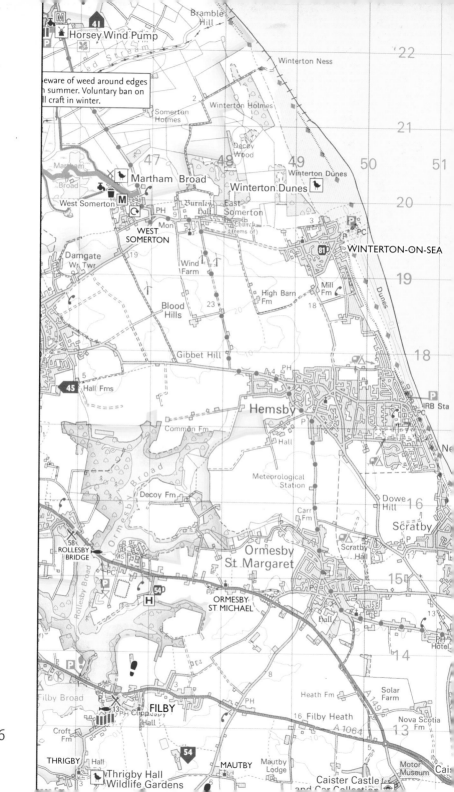

Horsey Wind Pump 41

Winterton Ness

'22

Bramble
Hill

d Stream

eware of weed around edges
n summer. Voluntary ban on
ll craft in winter.

Somerton
Holmes

Winterton Holmes

2

21

Decoy
Wood

Martham 47   48   49   50   51
Broad

Winterton Dunes

Martham Broad

Winterton Dunes   20

West Somerton   Burnley   East
Hall   Somerton

PH   Church   3   PC
9   (rems of)   P
Mon   R

**WEST
SOMERTON**   **WINTERTON-ON-SEA**   81

Damgate   19
Wr Twr   19
Wind   19
Farm

Blood   High Barn   Mill
Hills   23   Fm   Fm

20   18

Gibbet Hill   PH   18
4   18

45 Hall Frms   5   Hemsby

Common Fm

Broad   Hall   IRB Sta
PC

Ne

Meteorological
Station

Decoy Fm   Dowe
Hitt   16

Carr   Scratby
Fm   Hall
58   17   **Scratby**
**ROLLESBY
BRIDGE**   MS   Scratby
PC   Ormesby   Hall
**Ormesby
St Margaret**   15
Rollesby Broad   54   13
H   Hall
**ORMESBY
ST MICHAEL**   14

Solar   PH
Farm   Hotel
13

Filby Broad   Nova Scotia
MS   Heath Fm   Fm
13   Cloppesby   **FILBY**   A 149
PH   Hall   16 Filby Heath   Motor
Croft   A 1064   13   Museum
Fm   Cai

46   THRIGBY   Hall   54   MAUTBY   Mautby
Thrigby Hall   Lodge   Caister Castle
Wildlife Gardens

Horsey Wind Pump, one of the many picturesque mills seen around the Broads.

Pulls Ferry in central Norwich, was once a fifteenth century water gate and a canal ran under the arch that was used to take stone for building the cathedral. The ferry across the Wensum ran until 1948..

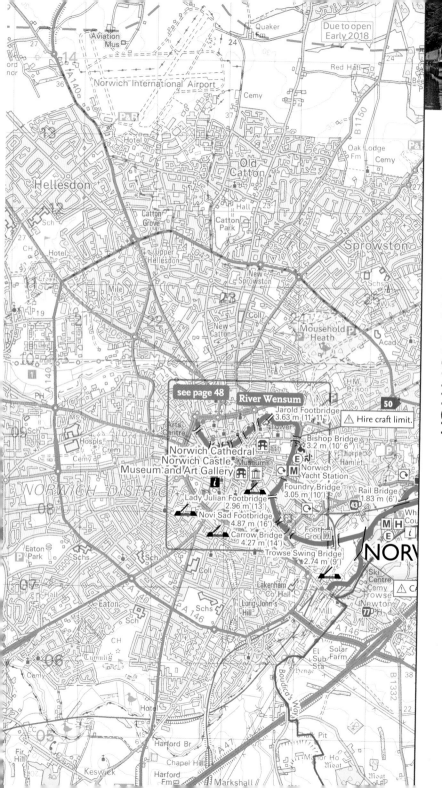

Due to open Early 2018

Norwich International Airport

see page 48 — River Wensum

Jarold Footbridge 3.63 m (11'11")

⚠ Hire craft limit.

Bishop Bridge 3.2 m (10' 6")

Norwich Cathedral
Norwich Castle
Museum and Art Gallery

Norwich Yacht Station

Foundry Bridge 3.05 m (10')

Rail Bridge 1.83 m (6')

Lady Julian Footbridge 2.96 m (13')

Novi Sad Footbridge 4.87 m (16')

Carrow Bridge 4.27 m (14')

Trowse Swing Bridge 2.74 m (9')

NORW

NORWICH DISTRICT

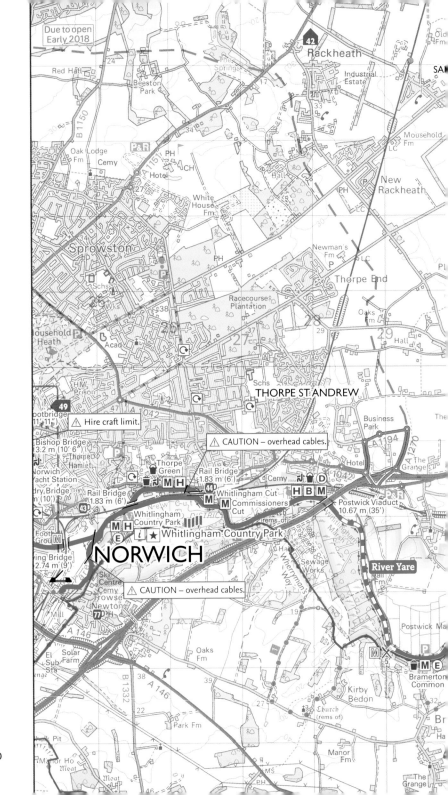

Due to open Early 2018

Rackheath

42

Red Hall

Beeston Park

SA

Industrial Estate

B 1150

Mousehold Fm

Oak Lodge Fm

Cemy

P&R

A 1151

PH

CH

Hotel

New Rackheath

LC

White House Fm

PH

P

Sprowston

PH

Newman's Fm

LC

Thorpe End

Schs

Racecourse Plantation

Oaks Fm

Hall

ousehold Heath

Acad

HM Prison

THORPE ST ANDREW

Business Park

49

A 1270

⚠ Hire craft limit.

A 1042

A 1194

The Grange

ootbridge 11' 11"

Bishop Bridge 3.2 m (10' 6")

⚠ CAUTION – overhead cables.

Hotel

A 1042

Norwich Yacht Station

Thorpe Hamlet

Thorpe Green

Rail Bridge 1.83 m (6')

Cemy

P&R

ry Bridge m (10')

Rail Bridge 1.83 m (6')

44

Whitlingham Cut Commissioners Cut

Postwick Viaduct 10.67 m (35')

43

Whitlingham Country Park

District

New Cut (rems of)

Foot Grou

★ Whitlingham Country Park

NORWICH

Sewage Works

River Yare

ing Bridge 2.74 m (9')

Centre Cemy Trowse Newton

⚠ CAUTION – overhead cables.

Wherryman's Way

77

PH

Postwick Ma

Mill

A 146

Oaks Fm

P

Bramerton Common

El Sub Sta

Solar Farm

5

Kirby Bedon

B 1332

A 146

38

39

Church (rems of)

22

Park Fm

Manor Fm

Br

Ha

Manor Ho Meat

The Grange

Strumpshaw Fen is an RSPB reserve. It has many interesting habitats including woodland, reedbeds and orchid-rich meadows. On a visit you may see marsh harriers, bitterns and kingfishers. In spring and summer there are dragonflies and butterflies. There are at least six types of orchids to be seen here. For details on places to visit *see* pages 86–95.

For more information on Wildlife of the Broads *see* page 76.

For more information on visiting Nature Reserves *see* page 90.

Kingfisher

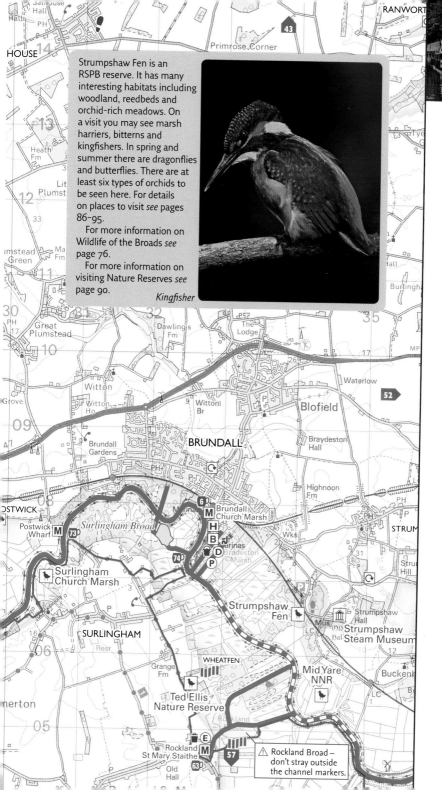

Primrose Corner

BRUNDALL

Witton
Witton Ho
Witton Br

Blofield

Brundall Gardens

Braydeston Hall

Highnoon Fm

POSTWICK

Postwick Wharf

Surlingham Broad

Brundall Church Marsh

Braydeston Marsh

STRUM

Surlingham Church Marsh

SURLINGHAM

Strumpshaw Fen

Strumpshaw Hall
Old Strumpshaw Hall Steam Museum

WHEATFEN

Grange Fm

Mid Yare NNR

Buckenh

Ted Ellis Nature Reserve

merton

Rockland St Mary Staithe
Old Hall

⚠ Rockland Broad – don't stray outside the channel markers.

RANWORTH **M** *i*
Ranworth Staithe
South Walsham
Broad

South Walsham

44

Upton
Fen
The D

Low Fm

Upton Broad

Upt

Upt
Gree

Fairhaven
Garden Trust

Hotel

Pilson
Green

SOUTH
WALSHAM

68

PH

69

Tyegate
Green

Panxworth

Hall

Town
Green

Hare Fen

Mill Hill
Fm

Cargate
Green

78

Upton

Highfield
Fm

Walsham
Wood

Hemb

gton

24

ebush
Fm

Sch

Wat

51

ofield

Cruiser moored on the River Bure

Braydeston
Hall

Highnoon
Fm

PH

LC

Resr

Church Fm

LC

18

Lingwood
Sch

23

PH

STRUMPSHAW

Old Hall
Fm

South
Burlingham

Lincoln Hall

Beighton

Moulton
St Mary

31

Strumpshaw
Hill

Cucumber
Corner

Ash Tre
Fn

Strumpshaw
Hall

Mus
Old Strumpshaw
Hall Steam Museum

LC

Mid Yare
NNR

Buckenham

Buckenham Carrs

Hassingham

PH

Hall
church
ems of)

Manor Fm

Hall

d Broad –
ay outside
nnel markers.

58

B

The Oaks

Spong
Carr

PH

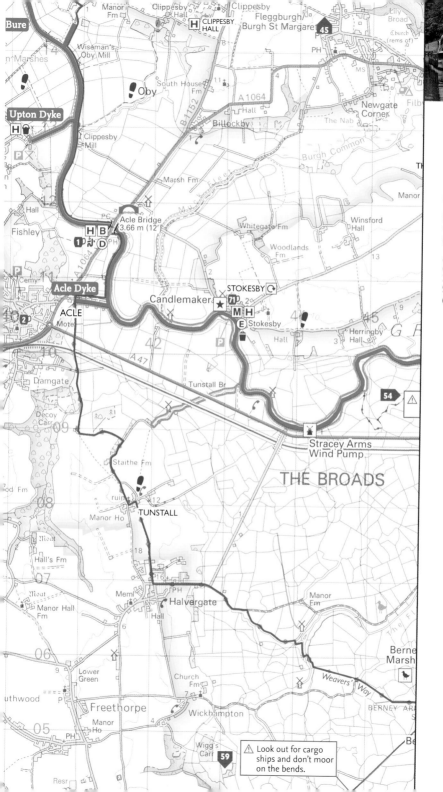

Bure

14

n'Marshes

Wiseman's
Oby Mill

Oby

South House
Fm

Manor
Fm

Clippesby
Hall

Clippesby

H CLIPPESBY
HALL

Fleggburgh
Burgh St Margaret

45

PH

Newgate
Corner

Lily
Broad

Church
(rems of)

Filb

Upton Dyke

H

P

Clippesby
Mill

Marsh Fm

B1152

Hall

Billockby

A1064

The Nab

Burgh Common

Manor

Fishley

Hall

Cemy

P

ACLE

Mote

10

Damgate

09

Decoy
Carr

Acle Bridge
3.66 m (12'

H B

D

PH

Acle Dyke

Candlemaker

A1064

A 47

42

Tunstall Br

Whitegate Fm

Woodlands
Fm

STOKESBY

71

M H

E Stokesby

Hall

P

Winsford
Hall

13

Herringby
Hall

45

G

54

od Fm

08

Staithe Fm

ruins

12

Manor Ho

TUNSTALL

Stracey Arms
Wind Pump

THE BROADS

Hall's Fm

07

Moat

Manor Hall
Fm

18

16

Mem

PH

Halvergate

Hall

Manor
Fm

Berne
Marsh

uthwood

06

Lower
Green

Freethorpe

Manor
Ho

05

Church
Fm

Wickhampton

Weavers' Way

BERNEY AR

Be

Wigg's
Carr

59

⚠ Look out for cargo
ships and don't moor
on the bends.

Resr

53

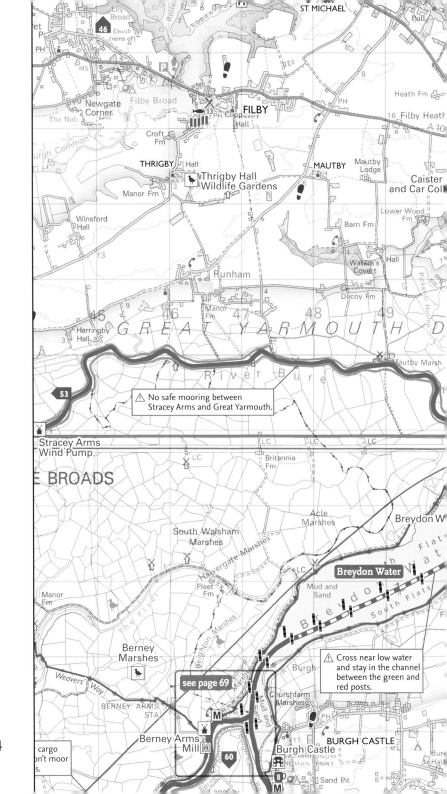

ST. MICHAEL

Heath Fm

46

Newgate
Corner

Church
(rems of)

Filby Broad

The Nab

MS

13 PH Clippesby
Hall

FILBY

16 Filby Heath

A 10

Croft
Fm

THRIGBY Hall

Thrigby Hall
Wildlife Gardens

MAUTBY

Mautby
Lodge

Caister
and Car Coll

Manor Fm

Winsford
Hall

13

Barn Fm

Lower Wood
Fm

Waters's
Covert Hall

Runham

Decoy Fm

45 16 47 48 49

G R E A T   Y A R M O U T H   D

Herringby
Hall

Manor
Fm

53

River Bure

Mautby Marsh

⚠ No safe mooring between
Stracey Arms and Great Yarmouth.

Stracey Arms
Wind Pump

LC LC LC

Britannia
Fm

E BROADS

South Walsham
Marshes

Acle
Marshes

Breydon W

Halvergate Marshes

LC

Breydon Water

Manor
Fm

Fleet
Fm

Mud and
Sand

South Flats

Breydon

The Fleet

Berney
Marshes

Burgh

⚠ Cross near low water
and stay in the channel
between the green and
red posts.

Weavers' Way

see page 69

Churchfarm
Marshes

BERNEY ARMS
STA

M

Berney Arms
Mill **M**

60

BURGH CASTLE

Burgh Castle
ROMAN FORT

Sand Pit

Bure

Hall

cargo
n't moor
s.

54

8
M

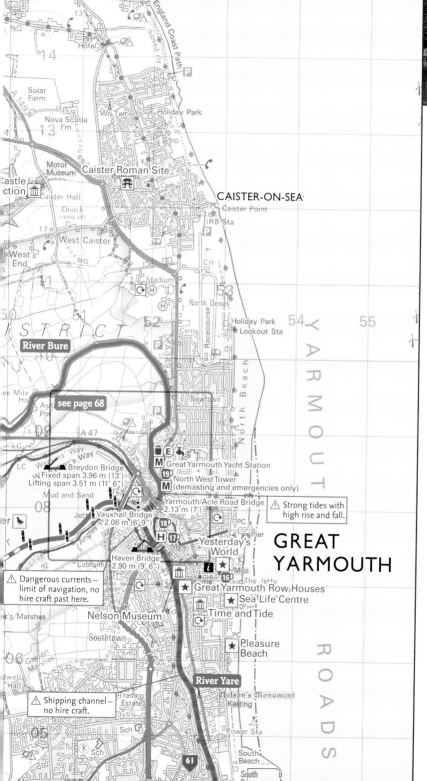

PC

13

PH Hotel

14

A 149

Solar Farm

Nova Scotia Fm

13

Motor Museum

Castle ction

Caister Hall

Caister Roman Site

Church (rems of)

17

West Caister

West End

West's Way

Wr Twr

Holiday Park

P

CAISTER-ON-SEA

Cemy

Caister Point

IRB Sta

P

CH

Stadium

North Denes

Holiday Park
Lookout Sta

Racecourse

54 55

Cemy

River Bure

STRICT

Three Mile Ho

Ash Fm

see page 68

Newtown

North Beach

A 47

P

Weavers' Way

West's Way

LC

E
M
Great Yarmouth Yacht Station

19
North West Tower
(demasting and emergencies only)
M

Breydon Bridge
Fixed span 3.96 m (13')
Lifting span 3.51 m (11' 6")

Mud and Sand

08

Jetty

Vauxhall Bridge
2.06 m (6', 9")

Yarmouth/Acle Road Bridge
2.13 m (7')

⚠ Strong tides with
high rise and fall.

Anglies

PC

18
H 17
Yesterday's
World

**GREAT
YARMOUTH**

Haven Bridge
2.90 m (9' 6")

Cobholm

⚠ Dangerous currents –
limit of navigation, no
hire craft past here.

Mus

Pier

The Jetty

★ Great Yarmouth Row Houses
★ Sea Life Centre
Time and Tide

's Marshes

Nelson Museum

Southtown

16

★ Pleasure
Beach

06 Gapton
Marshes

owell
Hall

⚠ Shipping channel –
no hire craft.

Trading
Estate

River Yare

Nelson's Monument
Karting

R O A D S

05

Sch

Sch

24

61

Power Sta

South
Beach

South
Denes

Reedham Chain Ferry is an important crossing point on the River Yare for cars and pedestrians. See also
Navigation Notes, page 17.

Reed and sedge has been cut and harvested in the Broads for centuries – the bundles of reed
were transported from the reed beds by boat, using the network of dykes and rivers, which
gave access to the nearby settlements. The reed was used to thatch buildings of all types,
including churches and barns. Other vegetation was cut as feed and bedding for animals.
The cutting process helped keep the traditional Broads landscape open by preventing the fens
becoming overgrown by scrub and woodland, and provided a natural habitat for wildlife and
plants. The commercial reed-cutting industry experienced a steady decline and had almost
died out when, with assistance from the Broads Authority, the Broads Reed and Sedge Cutters
Association (www.reedcutters.norfolkbroads.com) was formed in 2002.

This European award-winning project enabled the association to access grants for training
and cutting equipment, and has resulted
in new reed cutters taking up the trade.
It has also provided other work such as
coppicing and scrub clearance, which
helps provide the cutters with a stable
income throughout the year. Although
modern mowing equipment has been
developed, the trade is still harsh work
and labour intensive: reed is cut during
the winter months, once frosts have
removed the leaves from the reed
stems; and hand tools are still used in
vulnerable areas and during high tides.
Sedge, more flexible than reed, is cut
in the summer. Reed beds are now
being restored and reed is being cut
commercially on some sites for the first
time in many years.

A trainee reed cutter near Sutton, Norfolk.

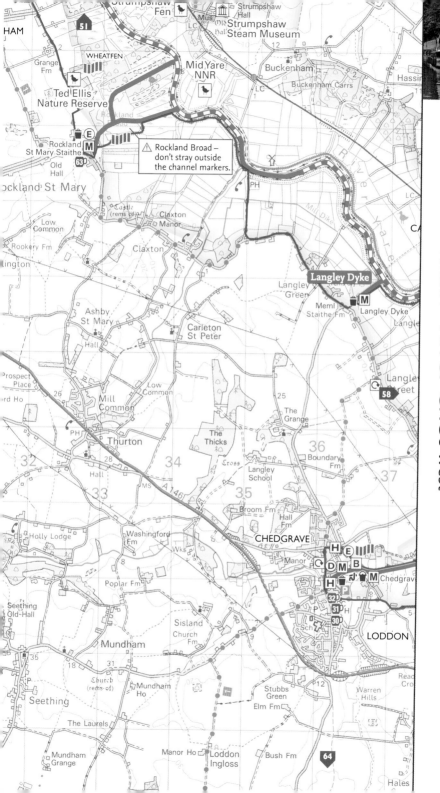

HAM

51

Strumpshaw Fen

Strumpshaw Hall

Strumpshaw Steam Museum

Mus

Old Strumpshaw Hall

12

WHEATFEN

Grange Fm

Mid Yare NNR

Buckenham

LC

Buckenham Carrs

Hassi

Ted Ellis Nature Reserve

Rockland

E
M

Rockland St Mary Staithe

63

Old Hall

⚠ Rockland Broad – don't stray outside the channel markers.

PH

River

Mill Dyke

River Yare

CA

ckland St Mary

Castle (rems of)

Claxton Manor

Claxton

Low Common

Rookery Fm

ington

Ashby St Mary

Hall

Carleton St Peter

Langley Dyke

Langley Green

Meml
Staithe Fm

M

Langley Dyke

Langle

Prospect Place

rd Ho

26

Mill Common

Low Common

25

The Grange

Langle reet

58

PH

Thurton

The Thicks

Cross

Langley School

36

Boundary Fm

37

32

28

34

35

33

Hall

MS

A146

Broom Fm

Hall Fm

CHEDGRAVE

Washingford Fm

Wks

Manor

H **E**

D **M** **B**

H

M

Chedgrav

Holly Lodge

Poplar Fm

8

P

32

Seething Old-Hall

Sisland Church Fm

31
30

PH

Sch

LODDON

Mundham

18

31

Church (rems of)

Mundham Ho

Stubbs Green

Elm Fm

12

Read Cro

Warren Hills

Seething

The Laurels

Mundham Grange

Manor Ho

Loddon Ingloss

Bush Fm

64

Hales

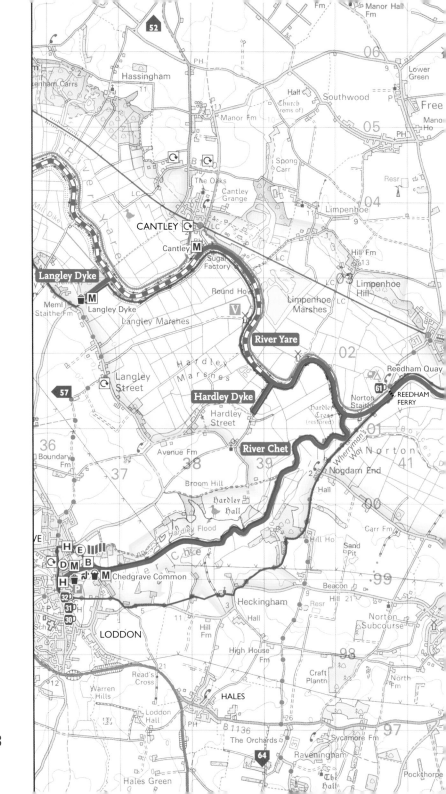

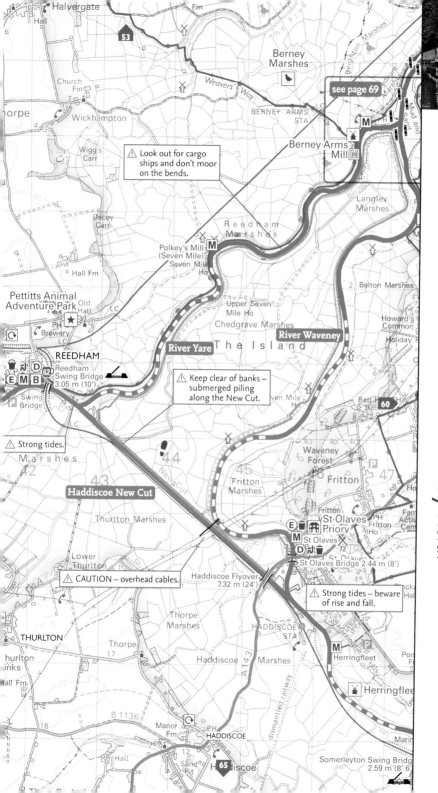

Halvergate

Hall

53

Fm

The Fleet

Berney
Marshes

Weavers' Way

Berghton Marshes

see page 69

BERNEY ARMS
STA

M

Church
Fm

Wickhampton

⚠ Look out for cargo
ships and don't moor
on the bends.

Berney Arms
Mill M

Mud and sand

horpe

Wigg's
Carr

Langley
Marshes

Decoy
Carr

Reedham
Marshes

Belton Marshes

Polkey's Mill
(Seven Mile)
Seven Mile
Ho

M

Hall Fm

Upper Seven
Mile Ho

Chedgrave Marshes

Howard's
Common

Holiday

Pettitts Animal
Adventure Park

Old
Hall

LC

River Waveney

River Yare The Island

↻ ⚓ 🍺 Brewery

REEDHAM

Seven Mile
Ho

Bell
Bath

60

J D

Reedham
Swing Bridge
3.05 m (10')

E M B

Swing
Bridge

⚠ Keep clear of banks –
submerged piling
along the New Cut.

P

LC

⚠ Strong tides.

Marshes
42

44

NewsCut

43

45

Waveney
Forest

46 Fritton 47

Haddiscoe New Cut

Fritton
Marshes

P

Ho

Thurlton Marshes

Fritton
St Olaves PH Fam
Activ
Cen

E 🏠

Lower
Thurlton

⚠ CAUTION – overhead cables.

St Olaves
Priory

Fritton
Ho

M St Olaves

D

St Olaves Bridge 2.44 m (8')

THURLTON

Thorpe
Marshes

Haddiscoe Flyover
7.32 m (24')

⚠ Strong tides – beware
of rise and fall.

ock
Hal

hurlton
inks

Thorpe
17

HADDISCOE
STA

Herringfleet

Pon

all Fm

B 1136

Haddiscoe

A143

Marshes

M

P

Herringfleet

Hills

18

Manor
Fm

↻

PH

dismantled railway

Herringflee

HADDISCOE

Hall

Sand
Pit

65 iscoe

12

Somerleyton Swing Bridg
2.59 m (8' 6'

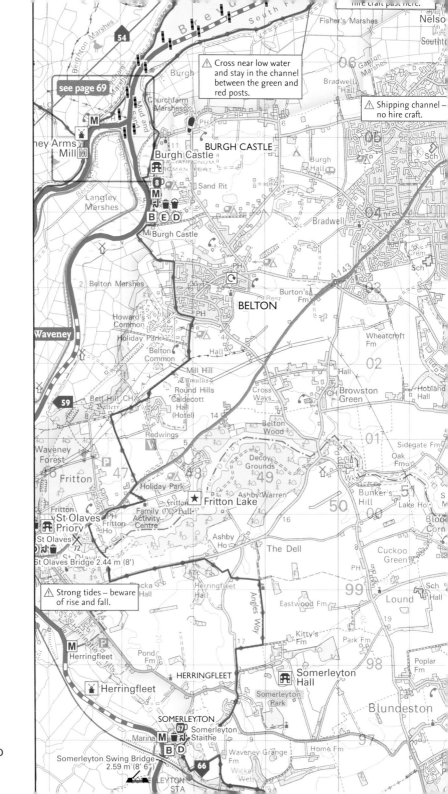

54

Fisher's Marshes Nelso

Southt

⚠ Cross near low water
and stay in the channel
between the green and
red posts.

Gapton
Marshes

Bradwell
Hall

⚠ Shipping channel –
no hire craft.

see page 69

Burgh

Churchfarm
Marshes

Mud and

Sch

M

ey Arms
Mill **M**

BURGH CASTLE

Burgh Castle
GARIANNONUM
ROMAN FORT

Burgh
Hall

Langley
Marshes

Sand Pit

Burgh Castle

Bradwell

M

B E D

Burgh Castle

Crem

Sch

A143

PH

BELTON

Burton's
Fm

Resr

PH

Waveney

Howard's
Common

Holiday Park

Belton
Common

Belton Marshes

Wheatcroft
Fm

Mill Hill

Hall

59

Tumulus

Round Hills
Caldecott
Hall
(Hotel)

Bett Hill CH
Battery

Cross
Ways

Belton
Wood

CH

Browston
Green

Hobland
Hall

Waveney
Forest

P

Redwings

Decoy
Grounds

Oak
Fm

Sidegate Fm

Fritton

46

47

48

49

50

51

Holiday Park

Ashby Warren

Bunker's
Hill

Lake Ho

Blood
Corn

Fritton

★ Fritton Lake

Fritton Old Hall

Fritton
Ho

Family
Activity
Centre

Ashby
Ho

16

The Dell

Cuckoo
Green

St Olaves
Priory

St Olaves

72

St Olaves Bridge 2.44 m (8')

⚠ Strong tides – beware
of rise and fall.

Herringfleet
Hall

Angles Way

Eastwood Fm

PH

Lound

Sch

Hall

99

M

Herringfleet

Pond
Fm

Kitty's
Fm

Park Fm

98

Poplar
Fm

Herringfleet

HERRINGFLEET

Somerleyton
Hall

Somerleyton
Park

Blundeston

97

SOMERLEYTON

67 Somerleyton
Staithe

Marina **M**

B D

Somerleyton Swing Bridge
2.59 m (8' 6")

66

LEYTON
STA

Waveney Grange
Fm

Wicker
Well

Home Fm

Museum
Time and Tide
PC
Pleasure Beach
55
ROADS
River Yare
Nelson's Monument
Karting
Trading Estate
Power Sta
Sch
South Beach
Cemy
Coll
South Denes
P
Lifeboat Sta
P
Lookout Sta
P
Gorleston-on-Sea
Gorleston Cliffs
spital
Sch
CH
16
52
67
all
an's
Im Fm

Somerleyton Hall is an excellent example of a Tudor-Jacobean mansion. There has been a building here since the post conquest Norman era. The Hall is open to the public. See Places to Visit, page 87.

PH
White House Fm
Corton
511
Hall
B1375
CORTON
Moat
A12
PH
Whitehouse
67
Pleasurewood Hills
1
Gunton Hall
P
Lowestoft North

Sailing on the River Waveney near Beccles.

Suffolk Wildlife Trust manages the five nature reserves which make up the Suffolk Broads; Carlton Marshes, Oulton Marshes, Castle Marshes, North Cove and Camps Heath can all be found on map page 66.

For more information on visiting Nature Reserves *see* page 90.

For more information on Wildlife of the Broads *see* page 76.

Short-eared owl.

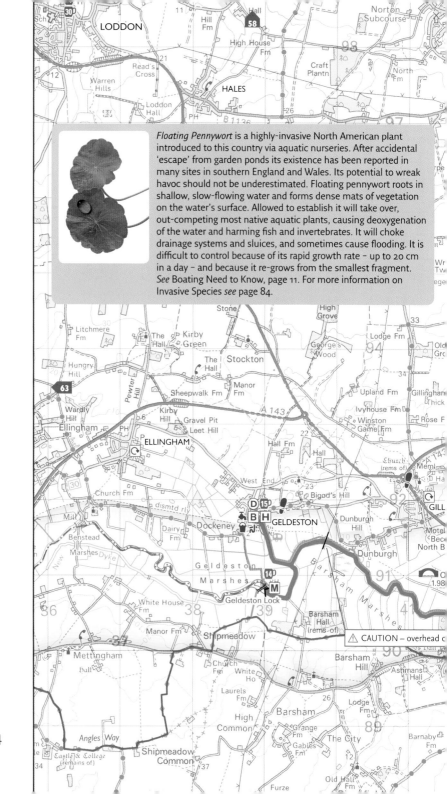

Floating Pennywort is a highly-invasive North American plant introduced to this country via aquatic nurseries. After accidental 'escape' from garden ponds its existence has been reported in many sites in southern England and Wales. Its potential to wreak havoc should not be underestimated. Floating pennywort roots in shallow, slow-flowing water and forms dense mats of vegetation on the water's surface. Allowed to establish it will take over, out-competing most native aquatic plants, causing deoxygenation of the water and harming fish and invertebrates. It will choke drainage systems and sluices, and sometimes cause flooding. It is difficult to control because of its rapid growth rate – up to 20 cm in a day – and because it re-grows from the smallest fragment. *See* Boating Need to Know, page 11. For more information on Invasive Species *see* page 84.

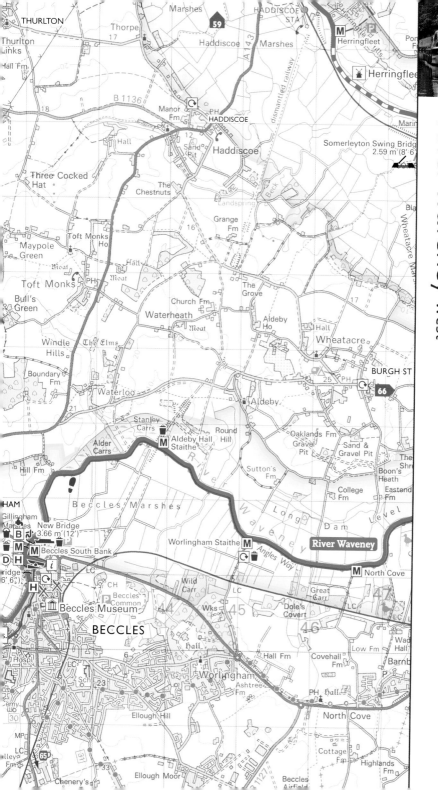

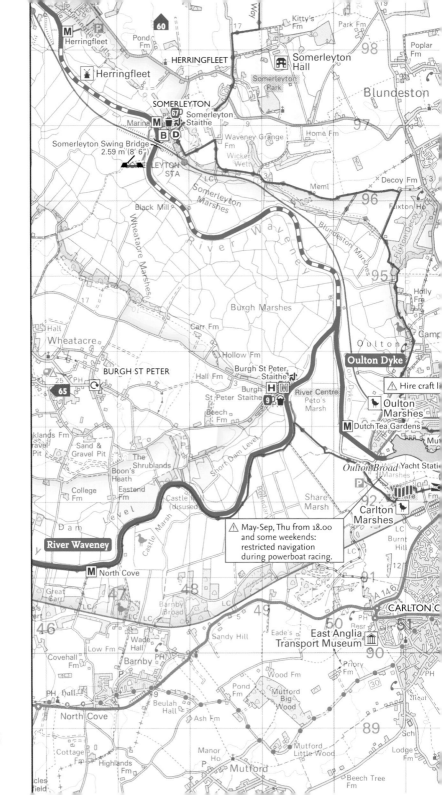

⚠ May-Sep, Thu from 18.00 and some weekends: restricted navigation during powerboat racing.

CORTON

Corton

Holiday Park

Water Treatment Works

White House Fm

Hall Moat

PH

Whitehouse Fm

Old Hall

PH

Hotel

Parkhill

PH

Sch

Manor Ho

Oulton

Gunton Hall

PC

Gunton

Pleasurewood Hills

North Beach

Maritime Museum

Lowestoft Maritime Museum

Normanston

Acad

Coll

Cemy

Dan Hill

Hosp

East Point Pavilion

Euroscope

Lowestoft Ness

Mutford Bridges
2.39 m (7'10")

Lowestoft Harbour Bridge
2.16 m (7'11")

Lowestoft Museum

Harbour

LB Sta

PC

LOWESTOFT

Claremont Pier

Kirkley

Wr Twr

Pakefield
Sch

Bloodmoor Hill

Ind Est

Grange Fm

Pakefield Hall

Lowestoft North Roads

The end of Claremont Pier at sunrise.

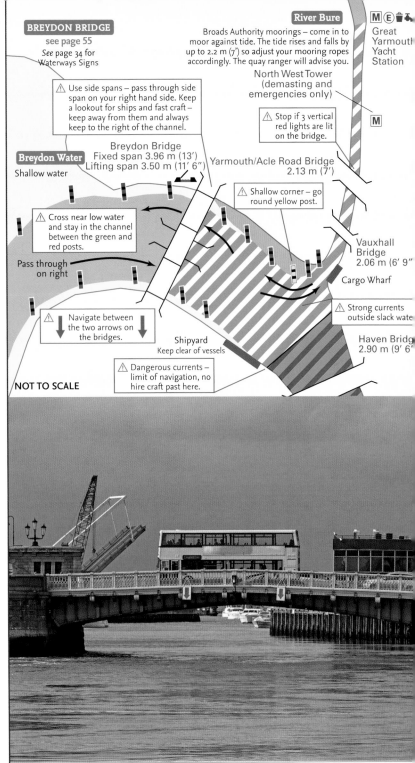

BREYDON BRIDGE

see page 55

See page 34 for Waterways Signs

River Bure

Ⓜ Ⓔ 🚽 🔧

Great Yarmouth Yacht Station

Broads Authority moorings – come in to moor against tide. The tide rises and falls by up to 2.2 m (7') so adjust your mooring ropes accordingly. The quay ranger will advise you.

⚠ Use side spans – pass through side span on your right hand side. Keep a lookout for ships and fast craft – keep away from them and always keep to the right of the channel.

North West Tower (demasting and emergencies only)

Ⓜ

⚠ Stop if 3 vertical red lights are lit on the bridge.

Breydon Water

Shallow water

Breydon Bridge
Fixed span 3.96 m (13')
Lifting span 3.50 m (11' 6")

Yarmouth/Acle Road Bridge
2.13 m (7')

⚠ Shallow corner – go round yellow post.

⚠ Cross near low water and stay in the channel between the green and red posts.

Vauxhall Bridge
2.06 m (6' 9"

Cargo Wharf

Pass through on right

⚠ Strong currents outside slack wate

Haven Bridg
2.90 m (9' 6'

⚠ Navigate between the two arrows on the bridges.

Shipyard
Keep clear of vessels

⚠ Dangerous currents – limit of navigation, no hire craft past here.

NOT TO SCALE

Haven Bridge, Great Yarmouth.

Breydon Water

⚠ Cross near low water and
stay in the channel
between the green and
red posts.

⚠ Turn left or right – DO
NOT go straight on or
you will run aground.

Berney Arms P.H. ■

M

Berney Arms Mill

M

River Yare

⚠ Shallow water
and mud.

Burgh Castle

River Waveney

NOT TO SCALE

Breydon Water

Burgh Castle roman fort. See *Places to Visit*, page 86.

	Bicycle	Boat trips	Canoes	Electric boats	Motor boats	Rowing boats	Sailing dinghies	Learn to Sail (S)	Canoe (C) Windsurf (W) Paddleboard (SUP)
Fritton Lake Fritton Lake Activity Centre (page 60) *Church Lane, Fritton, Great Yarmouth, Norfolk NR31 9HA (03334 560777; www.frittonlake.eoc.co.uk). No dogs allowed on site.*	✓		✓		✓	✓			✓(SUP)
Rollesby Broad The Waterside Rollesby (page 46) *Main Road, Rollesby, Norfolk NR29 5EF (01493 740531; www.thewatersiderollesby.co.uk). No dogs allowed on site.*		✓			✓	✓			
River Ant Bank Dayboats (page 39) *Staithe Cottage, Wayford Bridge, Norwich, Norfolk NR12 9LN (01692 582457; www.bankboats.co.uk)*			✓		✓				
Broadland Day Boats (page 44) *Ludham Bridge Boatyard, Ludham, Norfolk NR29 5NX (01692 667659; www.dayboathire.com)*			✓		✓				
Ludham Bridge Boatyard (page 44) *Johnson Street, Ludham, Norfolk NR29 5NX (01692 631011; www.ludhambridgeboats.co.uk)*	✓		✓				✓	✓	
Nancy Oldfield Trust (page 43) ⅃ *Irstead Road, Neatishead, Norwich, Norfolk NR12 8BJ (01692 630572; www.nancyoldfield.org.uk). Wheelchair accessible boat.*	✓	✓	✓	✓				✓	
Richardsons Cruisers (page 39) *The Staithe, Stalham, Norwich, Norfolk NR12 9BX (01692 668981; www.richardsonsboatingholidays.co.uk)*					✓				
Sutton Staithe Boatyard (page 39) *Sutton Staithe, Sutton, Norfolk NR12 9QS (01692 581653; www.suttonstaitheboatyard.co.uk)*			✓		✓				
River Bure Barnes Brinkcraft (page 42) *Riverside Road, Wroxham, Norwich, Norfolk NR12 8UD (01603 782625; www.barnesbrinkcraft.co.uk)*			✓		✓	✓	✓		

	Bicycle	Boat trips	Canoes	Electric boats	Motor boats	Rowing boats	Sailing dinghies	Learn to Sail (S) Canoe (C) Windsurf (W) Padleboard (SUP)
Boulter Marine Services (page 43) *Ferry View Road, Horning, Norfolk, Norfolk NR12 8PT (01692 630498; www.boultermarine.co.uk)*				✓	✓			
Bridgecraft (page 53) *Acle Bridge, Acle, Norwich, Norfolk NR13 3AS (01493 750378)*					✓			
Broadland Cycle Hire (page 43) *BeWILDerwood, Horning Road, Hoveton, Norwich NR12 8JW (07887 480331; www.norfolkbroadscycling.co.uk)*	✓							
Broads Tours (page 42) ♿ *The Bridge, Norwich Road, Wroxham, Norfolk NR12 8RX (01603 782207: www.broads.co.uk)*		✓		✓	✓			
Eastwood-Whelpton (page 53) *Upton Yacht Station, Upton, Norwich, Norfolk NR13 6BL (01493 750430; www.eastwood-whelpton.co.uk)*					✓	✓		✓(S)
Ferry Marina (page 43) ♿ *Ferry Road, Horning, Norwich, Norfolk NR12 8PS (01692 631111; www.ferry-marina.co.uk)*					✓			
Richardson's Day Boat Hire (page 42) *Fineway Leisure, The Rhond, Hoveton, Norfolk NR12 8UD (01603 782309; www.richardsonsboatingholidays.co.uk)*				✓	✓			
Horstead Centre (page 42) *(Residential outdoor centre) Rectory Road, Horstead, Norwich, Norfolk NR12 7EP (01603 737215; www. horsteadcentre.org.uk)*								✓(C)
JB Boat Sales (page 43) *106 Lower Street, Horning, Norwich, Norfolk NR12 8PF (01692 631411; wwww.jbboats.co.uk)*					✓			
King Line Cottages (page 43) ♿ *Ferry Road, Horning, Norwich, Norfolk NR12 8PS (01692 630297; www.norfolk-broads.co.uk). Electric boat hire for the disabled & elderly.*				✓				

River Bure (continued)

	Bicycle	Boat trips	Canoes	Electric boats	Motor boats	Rowing boats	Sailing dinghies	Learn to Sail (S)	Canoe (C) Windsurf (W) Padleboard (SUP)
Mississippi River Boats (page 43) ♿ *The Swan Hotel, Lower Street, Horning, Norfolk NR12 8AA (01692 630262; www.southern-comfort.co.uk)*		✓							
Riverside Tearooms and Stores (page 53) *The Green, Stokesby, Great Yarmouth, Norfolk NR29 3EX (01493 750470; www.stokesby.org.uk/page14.html).*	✓								
Salhouse Broad (page 43) *Lower Street, Salhouse, Norwich, Norfolk NR13 6RX (01603 722775/07795 145475; www.salhousebroad.org.uk)*			✓						
Wherry Yacht Charter (page 42) *The Wherry Base, Barton House, Hartwell Road, Wroxham, Norfolk NR12 8TL (01692 630674; www.wherryyachtcharter.org)*								✓(S)	

River Chet

	Bicycle	Boat trips	Canoes	Electric boats	Motor boats	Rowing boats	Sailing dinghies	Learn to Sail (S)	Canoe (C) Windsurf (W) Padleboard (SUP)
Pacific Cruisers (page 57) *Riverside, Pits Lane, Chedgrave, Loddon, Norfolk NR14 6NQ (01508 520321; www.pacificcruisers.co.uk)*					✓				

River Thurne

	Bicycle	Boat trips	Canoes	Electric boats	Motor boats	Rowing boats	Sailing dinghies	Learn to Sail (S)	Canoe (C) Windsurf (W) Padleboard (SUP)
Herbert Woods/Broads Tours (page 45) *Broads Haven Marina, Potter Heigham, Norfolk NR29 5JF (01692 670711/0800 144 4472; www.broads.co.uk)*		✓	✓	✓					
Hunter's Yard (page 44) *Horsefen Road, Ludham, Norfolk NR29 5QG (01692 678263; www.huntersyard.co.uk)*							✓	✓(S)	
Martham Boats (page 45) *Valley Works, Cess Road, Martham, Great Yarmouth, Norfolk NR29 4RF (01493 740249; www.marthamboats.com)*			✓		✓	✓	✓		✓(SUP)
Maycraft (page 45) *North West River Bank, Potter Heigham, Great Yarmouth, Norfolk NR29 5ND (01692 670241; www.maycraft.co.uk)*					✓				
Norfolk Broads School of Sailing (page 40) *Upton Yacht Station, Upton Acle NR13 6BL (01493 750430; www.norfolksailingschool.co.uk).*								✓(S)	

	Bicycle	Boat trips	Canoes	Electric boats	Motor boats	Rowing boats	Sailing dinghies	Learn to Sail (S) Canoe (C) Windsurf (W) Padleboard (SUP)
Norfolk Wherry Trust Forsythe Wherry Yard, Horsefen Road, Ludham, Great Yarmouth, Norfolk NR29 5QG (01603 473157; www.wherryalbion.com).								✓(S)
Phoenix Fleet (page 45) Repps Staithe Boatyard, Bridge Road, Potter Heigham, Great Yarmouth, Norfolk NR29 5JY (01692 670460; www.phoenixfleet.com)			✓	✓	✓			
Whispering Reeds (page 40) Staithe Road, Hickling, Norwich, Norfolk NR12 0YW 01692 596314; www.whisperingreeds.net)			✓		✓	✓	✓	
River Waveney CC Marine (page 65) 35 Northgate, Beccles, Suffolk NR34 9AU (01502 713703; www.ccmarinebeccles.co.uk)					✓			
H E Hipperson (page 65) Hipperson Boatyard, Gillingham Dam, Beccles, Suffolk NR34 0EB (01502 712166; www.hipppersons.co.uk)				✓	✓			
Oulton Broad Day Boats (page 67) 6 Yacht Station, Bridge Road, Lowestoft, Suffolk, NR33 9JS (01502 589556; www.waveneyrivertours.com)		✓			✓			
Outney Meadow Caravan Park (page 63) Outney Meadow, Bungay, Suffolk NR35 1HG (01986 892338; www.outneymeadow.co.uk)	✓		✓					
Rowancraft (page 65) Big Row, Geldeston, Beccles, Suffolk NR34 0LY (01508 518598/518208; www.rowancraft.com)				✓	✓			
Waveney River Centre (page 65) Sraithe Road, Burgh St Peter, Beccles, Suffolk NR34 0BT (01502 677343; www.waveneyrivercentre.co.uk)			✓		✓	✓		
Waveney River Tours (page 67) ♿ Mutford Lock Bridge Road, Oulton Broad, Lowestoft, Suffolk NR33 9JS (01502 574903; www.lovelowestoft.co.uk)		✓						

	Bicycle	Boat trips	Canoes	Electric boats	Motor boats	Rowing boats	Sailing dinghies	Learn to Sail (s) / Canoe (C) / Windsurf (W) / Paddleboard (SUP)
River Waveney (continued)								
Waveney Sailability (page 67) ♿ Oulton Broad Water Sports Centre, Nicholas Everitt Park, Oulton Broad, Lowestoft, Suffolk NR33 9JR (01502 587163; www.waveneysailability.co.uk)								✓(S)
Waveney Stardust (page 65) ♿ Georgian House, 34 Thoroughfare, Halesworth, Suffolk, IP19 8AP (07817 920502; www.waveneystardust.co.uk). Boat suitable for the elderly and disabled.		✓						
River Yare								
Freedom Boating Holidays Kingfisher Boatyard, Bungalow Lane, Norwich, Norfolk NR7 0SH (01603 858453; www.freedomboatingholidays.co.uk)			✓		✓			
Whitlingham Great and Little Broads								
Whitlingham Outdoor Education Centre (page 50) Whitlingham Lane, near Trowse, Norwich NR14 8TR (01603 756094/632307; www.norfolk.gov.uk)	✓		✓				✓	✓(SUP)
Near the Rivers Bure and Thurne								
Clippesby Hall (page 45) Clippesby, Norfolk NR29 3BL (01493 367800; www.clippesby.com/cyclehire.asp)	✓							
Around the Norfolk Broads								
The Canoe Man provides canoe hire, training and guided canoe trails through the Broads. Contact: 10 Norwich Road, Wroxham, Norwich, Norfolk NR12 8RX (0845 496 9177; www.thecanoeman.co.uk)			✓					✓(C)
HOLIDAY HIRE **Boat booking agencies**								
Blakes Holiday Boating Contact: Spring Mill, Stoneybank Road, Earby, Barnoldswick, Lancashire BB94 0AA (0345 498 6184; www.blakes.co.uk)					✓			
Hoseasons Boating Holidays Contact: Lowestoft, Suffolk NR32 2LW (0345 498 6589; www.hoseasons.co.uk/boat-holidays/)					✓			

Independent boatyards

As well as the booking agencies, these independent boatyards offer boating holidays on the Broads:

Freedom Boating Holidays *Kingfisher Boatyard, Bungalow Lane, Norwich, Norfolk NR7 oSH (01603 858453; www.freedomboatingholidays.co.uk)*

Maffett Cruisers *Pits Lane, Chedgrave, Loddon, Norwich, Norfolk NR14 6NQ (01508 520344; www.maffett-cruisers.com)*

Posh Boats *Ferry Marina, Ferry Road, Horning, Norfolk NR12 8PS (01692 631111; www.poshboats.co.uk)*

And also the following, all found in the listings above: Eastwood-Whelpton, Herbert Woods, Hunter's Yard, Martham Boats, Norfolk Wherry Trust, Wherry Yacht Charter, Pacific Cruisers.

Broads Authority Yacht Stations

Great Yarmouth Yacht Station (page 55) *Tar Works Road, Great Yarmouth, Norfolk NR30 1QX (01493 842794/07766 398238). Staffed Apr-Oct 08.00-20.00.* Moorings, help and advice.

Norwich Yacht Station (page 50) *Riverside Road, Norwich, Norfolk NR1 1SQ (01603 612980). Staffed Apr-Oct 08.00-20.00.* Moorings, pump out, help and advice.

Reedham Quay (page 59) *Reedham, Norfolk NR13 3TX (01493 701867). Staffed Apr-Oct 09.00-18.00.* Moorings, help and advice.

There are also yacht stations at
Beccles NR34 9BH (page 65 – 01502 712225) and
Oulton Broad NR33 9JS (page 67 – 01502 574946, VHF channel 73) on the River Waveney

♿ Wheelchair accessible –please contact the companies for further information.

The Broads contain a variety of differing habitats, supporting diverse species of wildlife. This unique wetland of rivers and Broads is surrounded by semi-natural habitats: fen, carr woodland and grazing marsh.

There is a natural change (if allowed to take place) from an area of open water to woodland. Fen is the first stage in this succession: waterlogged areas dominated by reeds, rushes and sedges. In spite of a significant loss of fen to woodland in the Broads since the early 19th century, there are about 1,700 ha (4,200 acres) of open fen – the largest expanses of species-rich fen in lowland Britain.

When fen is left unmanaged, small shrubs and trees start to grow, creating carr woodland. There are around 3,000 ha (7,413 acres) of woodland and scrub in the Broads, a third of which has developed during the past 50 years or so. Mature carr woodland is the most valuable: a tangle of woody species, shade-tolerant and low growing plants such as alder, sallow and birch trees, guelder rose, buckthorn, dog rose and brambles, ferns, mosses, lichen and fungi.

The Broads have had areas of grazing marsh since the 13th century, when sheep were grazed and marsh reclamation started. This trend continued through to the 20th century, at each stage drainage becoming more efficient and flooding become rarer. Today the grazing marshes support internationally and nationally important populations of wintering wildfowl, as well as raptors and breeding waders, and a host of invertebrate and plant communities. Skylarks are numerous, together with yellow wagtails and meadow pipits. Barn owls, short-eared owls, kestrels and occasionally marsh harriers feed on the abundant supply of small mammals.

A pioneering study commissioned by the Broads Authority and carried out by the University of East Anglia reveals that this small area, which makes up just 0.4% of the UK, is a haven for an incredible 25% of Britain's rarest species.

In an 322 sq mile area, the study identified 11,000 species, of which 66 are special to the Broads and 31 are rarely seen elsewhere in Britain. They include the Swallowtail Butterfly, Norfolk Hawker Dragonfly – the symbol of the Broads Authority – Holly-leave Naiad, Common Crane, and the Little Ramshorn Whirlpool Snail. This is due to a number of factors, including the presence of water, with large rivers flowing to the sea, and the wet peat soils.

However, one of the most significant factors is people. People have been managing the Broads for centuries, digging peat, cutting reed beds, excavating drains, managing water levels and creating places for wildlife.

Species that have recovered in number in recent years include the Crane, Otter, Bittern and Marsh Harrier. However, the research reveals that 423 rare species, including plants, insects and fish have disappeared in the last 23 years and 67 of these are known to have become extinct.

The following pages describe just a small selection of the wildlife to be seen in the Broads. Take a good guide with you when you visit the area (such as one of the Collins wildlife guides). Spend some time at one of the nature reserves (see Places to Visit, page 90), or contact the Broads Authority (see page 24) for details of activities designed to introduce visitors to the unique natural environment of the Broads. At the end of the chapter, we have included a list of some invasive species – the non-native creatures and plants that threaten the natural and native environment.

BIRDS
The Broads is renowned for many different bird species.

Bearded tit The bearded tit is one of several birds particularly associated with the Broads. It is an elusive species living in dense reedbeds where it feeds on insects, especially the larvae of moths, also spiders and seeds. It is usually seen in small groups, clambering up the reeds or flying, one after the other. Its call is a loud ching-ching. In some years, when numbers have built up, it 'erupts' and spreads to new areas. However, a severe winter can drastically reduce populations. Nests are built among the reeds. The bearded tit grows to 16–17 cm (6–6.5 inches) and has a long tail and mainly sandy-brown plumage; the male has a blue-grey head and conspicuous black 'moustaches'.

Bewick's swan The smallest British swan – it is a winter visitor between October and March from Siberian breeding grounds. The adults are pure white with a black and yellow bill, triangular in profile and barely reaching the nostrils. Juveniles have pinkish buff plumage and a pinkish bill: they arrive in Britain and remain together as family parties among larger flocks. Most birds return to traditional wintering sites and internationally important flocks of Bewick's swans have been recorded on Breydon Water.

Bittern The bittern is another bird species especially associated with the Broads. Deterioration of water quality and fenland habitat during the 20th century saw a sharp decline in numbers, but the Broads authority have been active in restoring habitats suitable for the bittern. The birds are seldom seen on account of their retiring nature and excellent camouflage afforded by the streaked buffish brown plumage in their favoured reedbed habitat. Their presence is often indicated by the male's loud booming call, uttered at dusk and through the night from April to June. When seen resting, the bird has a dumpy, hunched appearance. If alarmed, however, it adopts an upright, sky-pointing posture with its neck outstretched and the dagger-like bill held vertically. It will occasionally be seen briefly in flight, flying low over the tops of reeds on broad, rounded wings, with legs trailing. It grows to 70–80 cm (27.5–31.5 inches) and feeds mainly on fish and amphibians, but will take small waterside mammals too.

Long-tailed tit A charming resident of woods, heaths and hedgerows, feeding flocks resemble animated feather dusters. Outside the breeding season, the birds roost communally. These tits have a tiny, almost spherical body and a very long tail, with a small, stubby bill. Their plumage can look black and white, but at close range they have a pinkish wash to the underparts and are pinkish buff on the back. Their beautiful domed nests are built of moss, lichen and spider's webs.

Marsh harrier Another bird particularly connected with the Broads area and one that has made a successful comeback in recent times thanks to improved fen management. This rare bird is associated with wetlands, particularly extensive reedbeds. It flies at a slow speed just above the tops of the reeds, occasionally stalling to drop on prey. It is long-winged, with a wingspan of 110-125 cm (43-49 inches), and long-tailed. The male is reddish brown except for its blue-grey head and grey, unbarred tail; in flight, it has grey and reddish brown areas on the wings and black wingtips. The female is dark brown, except for a pale leading edge to the wing, and pale cap and chin. The nest is a pile of reeds and sticks on marshy ground.

Reed warbler As the name suggests, almost always associated with reedbeds. A common visitor from May-August. These singing birds 12-13 cm (5 inches) long, clamber up reeds or occasionally use bushes to deliver grating, chattering song that includes some mimetic elements. They have rather nondescript sandy-brown upperparts, paler underparts and dark legs. Nests are woven and cup-shaped, attached to upright reed stems. Reed warblers feed on insects.

Treecreeper A woodland bird, unobtrusive and easily overlooked as it creeps like a mouse up tree-trunks and larger branches. It typically feeds by spiralling round and up a tree, then dropping down to the base of an adjacent trunk to repeat the process – it will be searching for insects and spiders and, in winter, some seeds. It has streaked brown upperparts, pale underparts and a needle-like, downcurved bill, and is 12-13 cm (5 inches) long. The spiky tail is used as support when climbing. Its nest is built in a crevice, often behind loose bark.

Wigeon A scarce breeding species but locally common winter visitor to Britain. Breydon Water shelters nationally important wintering flocks. The male has an orange-red head with yellow forehead, pinkish breast and otherwise finely marked, grey plumage, with a characteristic black and white stern. In flight, the male has a bold white wing patch. The reddish brown female is best told by association with the male. The male's wheeoo call is evocative of winter estuaries.

Willow tit An inhabitant of the Broad's swampy carr woodland. It is similar in appearance to the marsh tit and is best identified by its nasal tchay tchay tchay call. The pale patch on its wing is not always distinguishable. It has a large head, pale wing-panel, dull black crown and a square-ended tail and is around 11-12 cm (4-5 inches) long. Its bill is small and black. The usual nest site is a hole excavated in a rotten tree stump. Willow tits feed on insects and seeds.

FISH

The Broads support a wide variety of fish species and offer wonderful opportunities for fishing (see Angling, page 20).

Bream A large 80 cm (31.5 inches) long, deep-bodied fish found in slow-moving rivers and brackish waters – large shoals are found throughout the Broads area. The fish feeds on invertebrates sucked from mud on the river bottom forming 'bream pits'. Bream are grey-brown above, silvery below on their sides. Larger fish may have a bronze tinge. They breed between April and June, spawning at night in shallow waters over vegetation such as weeds. Up to 340,000 yellowish eggs are laid and these hatch after about two weeks.

Perch A popular sport fish making a comeback to the waters of the Broads after a disease that decimated them during the 1970s. Perch inhabit lakes and slow rivers, often sheltering near roots, under overhanging trees, in deep reeds or under permanent moorings. They are dark green above, lighter below, with lateral lines on their sides. The two prominent dorsal fins are close together, with a dark blotch at the base of the first dorsal fin. The pelvic and anal fins are reddish. They grow to around 50 cm (19.5 inches). Spawning in late April–May, up to 200,000 pale yellowish eggs are laid over weed, appearing as long white strands.

Pike Commonplace throughout the Broads, this delicate species requires specialist tackle and skillful handling, in spite of its ferocious looks. It is a large predator – males averaging 90 cm (35.5 inches) long, females 150 cm (59 inches) – with a long snout and jaws and powerful teeth. Coloured olive green above and white or yellow below. The distinctive patterns on the sides are unique to larger specimens. The pike hunts alone, among vegetation, waiting motionless to pounce on prey: usually other fish but sometimes small mammals and young water birds. Spawning takes places in spring. Up to 500,000 tiny, yellowish eggs, in clusters of oil droplets are laid on vegetation in shallow water, hatching after 10–15 days.

Rudd Still common in the Broads waters, despite increasing scarcity throughout other parts of the country. Rudd are a shoal fish, preferring thick, reedy lakes and slow rivers. Similar in appearance to the roach, the rudd has a deep, flat-sided body, around 35–40 cm (14–16 inches), with its dorsal fin far back, and a jutting bottom jaw. Its back is coloured bluish-green, fading to a deep gold at the flank, and is silvery-white underneath. The fins are a deep orange; eyes are yellow-orange. Spawning takes place April–June. The eggs laid in large mats attached to reed stems and hatch after about seven days.

INSECTS

The increasingly good condition of the water in the Broads has lead to a much improved biodiversity, leading to more plants and insects, which in turn has led to an increased number of bird and fish species.

Comma butterfly Recognised by its distinctive ragged-edged wings, span 45 mm (2 inches) and smoky-brown underwings, with a white 'comma' mark; the upperwings are orange-brown with dark markings. It is double-brooded and hibernates. Flies March–September. The caterpillars feed on common nettle, elm and hops.

Common darter One of the most common dragonflies in England and Wales. The mature male has a blood-red abdomen, although in immature males and females this is orange-brown. The nymph is found among pondweed and debris. It frequently rests on the ground, but also uses perches. The common darter flies June–late autumn, often the latest flying species of dragonfly.

Banded demoiselle An attractive damselfly, often found resting among waterside vegetation. The males can be seen in small fluttering groups hovering over water while the flight of the female is rather feeble. They favour clean streams where the nymphs live partly buried in muddy sediment. The male has a blue body with a metallic sheen, the smoky wings show a conspicuous blue 'thumbprint' mark. The female has a green body with a metallic sheen and greenish brown wings. They grow to around 45 mm (2 inches) long. Flies May–August.

Glow worm The grub-like, wingless females, 14 mm (0.5 inches) long, may be located after dark by a greenish light emitted from the underside of tip to abdomen. This serves to attract winged males. The females will usually climb up grass stems and their luminosity ceases temporarily if they are disturbed. The adults do not feed, but the larvae, which can also emit light, eat snails. They may be found in meadows and along forest rides and verges.

Norfolk hawker dragonfly A rarity, one of two brown hawker dragonflies found in the United Kingdom, and restricted to the Broads fens and grazing marshes – it is the emblem of the Broads Authority. It has clear, untinted wings, green eyes and a yellow triangular mark on the second abdominal segment. Flies mainly June–July, although it can sometimes be seen through to early August.

Swallowtail butterfly Britain's largest butterfly, with a wingspan of around 70 mm (3.75 inches), unmistakable and rare, now confined to the wetlands of the Broads. Ragged robin and meadow thistle, found growing in the Broads fens, provide a vital food source, and milk parsley provides food for the caterpillars. The swallowtail flies between May and June, and again in August. Hickling Broad is a good place to look for the swallowtail, as is Strumpshaw Fen and How Hill (see Places to Visit, page 86).

MAMMALS
The various differing habitats of the Broads provide good conditions for many mammals.

Brown hare Formerly widespread and common, but has declined in many areas, in part due to persecution but also because of changes in land use. They are found in the Broads area, particularly on the grazing marshes. The brown hare is larger, longer legged and has longer, black-tipped ears than a rabbit. The males chase and box one another in spring.

Daubenton's bat A medium-sized bat with comparatively short ears. It is frequently associated with water and seen flying low over lakes, ponds and canals just as dusk is falling. It also feeds along woodland rides. Chirps can be heard by those with good hearing. It roosts in summer, sometimes in colonies, in hollow trees and tunnel entrances. In winter it hibernates.

Harvest mouse Britain's smallest rodent. It has orange-brown fur and is mainly nocturnal. Its presence is usually indicated by tennis ball-sized nests of woven grasses constructed among plant stems. The prehensile tail is almost as long as its body and is used when climbing among plant stems.

Otter The river corridors of the Broads are an important habit for otters and the Broads Authority has strict operating procedures to avoid disturbing them. The otter is superbly adapted to an amphibious lifestyle and its dives may last for several minutes. It feeds mainly on fish. Persecution from fishing interests, hunting and habitat destruction have caused a serious decline in numbers, but otters are increasingly seen in the Broads, following reintroduction efforts by the Otter Trust at Earsham.

Red deer An imposing animal and Britain's largest native land mammal. The male is larger that the female and has well developed, branching antlers. These are shed each February, reappear in the spring and become larger with each successive season. The summer coat is reddish brown but appears more grey-brown in winter; the underparts and rump are lighter. Red deer live in separate sex herds for much of the year and spend much of the daytime resting or wallowing in mud. They are most active from dusk to dawn. The annual autumn rut is accompanied by roaring, bellowing sounds from the stags. Chinese water deer and Muntjac deer are now becoming more common throughout the Broads.

Water vole Found in the dykes within the Broads, but have become rather scare in other areas due to habitat loss and predation by mink. These charming waterside mammals will dive into the water if danger threatens – they swim well both on the water's surface and underwater. The burrow complex usually has at least one submerged entrance. They grow to 18-22 cm (7-8.5 inches) long.

PLANTS
The Broads is one of the most wildlife-rich areas of all the country's national parks – the fens alone support more than 250 plant species.

Crested buckler fern Found in wet heaths, marshes and fens. Fronds are narrow and 2-times pinnately divided, arranged in a ladder-like pattern, growing up to 1 m (3 feet) tall.

Cross-leaved heath A downy, grey-green undershrub, growing up to 30 cm (12 inches) in height. It favours damp, acid soils, typical of boggy-margins on heaths and moors, and is widespread on the fens. The narrow leaves are in whorls of four along the stems. Pink flowers 5-6 cm (2 inches) long, are borne in terminal clusters from June-October.

Early marsh-orchid Found in damp meadows, often on calcareous soils but also acid conditions, growing up to 60 cm (23.5 inches) tall. The leaves are unmarked, yellowish green and narrow-lanceolate. The flowers are usually flesh-pink but can range from almost white to purple. The three-lobed flower lip is strongly reflexed along the mid-line. Flowers are borne on open spikes, May-June.

Grey willow Also known as grey sallow, this tree is named for the ash-coloured hairs which densely cover the young twigs and the underside of the broad oval leaves. The leaves develop inrolled margins with age. It is common to wet habitats and forms a broad crown in mature specimens. The catkins appear before the leaves, between March and April.

Guelder rose This shrub, or small tree, grows up to 4 m (13 feet) high. The leaves are divided into five, irregularly-toothed lobes. Flowers appear June–July in flat-topped heads, the inner ones much smaller then the outer ones. The berries are red.

Ragged robin A widespread and common perennial of damp meadows, marshes and the Broads fens. The narrow, grass-like leaves are rough, the upper ones in opposite pairs. The delicate-looking flowers comprise five pink petals each of which is divided into four lobes and they appear May–July. Ragged robin is an important food source for the swallowtail butterfly.

Meadow thistle A perennial of damp meadows, locally common in south and central England, Wales and Ireland, and found in the Broads fens, where it provides food for the swallowtail butterfly. The stem is unwinged, downy and ridged. Oval, toothed leaves are green and hairy above and white cottony below. The flower heads, 20–25 mm (1 inch) across, appear between June and July – reddish-purple florets and darker bracts on solitary heads.

Yellow water lily Water plant with oval, floating leaves, 20–30 cm (8–12 inches) across. Widespread and locally common. This water lily favours still or slow-moving water and roots in mud in the shallows. The flowers, carried on stalks, are 50–60 cm (19.5–23.5 inches) across and appear June–September.

INVASIVE SPECIES

There is a real and serious threat to both the environment and our native wildlife from non-native species. In recent years certain invasive non-native species have become a problem in and alongside the UK's canals and rivers. Within the Broads, as with other inland waterways, the non-native species cause extensive damage by changing natural habitats, making them unsuitable for local species and, sometimes, displacing them entirely.

Problem-causing plants include Japanese knotweed (see below), Himalayan balsam and giant hogweed. They quickly come to dominate riverbanks and exclude the native plants. Floating pennywort (see page 64), water fern and parrot's feather are water plants which choke drains and rivers, causing problems to navigation, nature conservation and flood management. The American signal crayfish carry a disease which kills our native white-clawed crayfish, and American mink threaten the Broad's water vole population. Foreign molluscs, such as the zebra mussel and the Asiatic clam block pipework and water intakes and have a negative impact on native mussels.

The Broads Authority monitors known problem sites and actively keeps a look out for fresh infestations. Please report any sightings of these or other non-native species to the Broads Authority or the Environment Agency (for contact details see page 24).

For more information, visit the website of the GB Non-Native Species Secretariat at www.nonnativespecies.org.

American mink An unwelcome alien which has become established after escaping from fur farms during the past few decades and is now established throughout the UK. The dark brown fur makes confusion with the otter possible, but the mink's smaller size 30–47 cm (12–18.5 inches), slimmer build and proportionally shorter tail help distinguish it. The American mink usually has white patches on its chin and throat, and small amounts of white fur may be present on the upper lip. It is invariably associated with water, particularly rivers and lakes, where it feeds on water birds, fish and waterside small mammals – it poses significant threat to the water vole population in the Broads.

Himalayan balsam was introduced from the Himalayas as a garden plant in the early 19th century. It is widely naturalised along river banks and on damp wasteground. It has small, explosive seeds, by which it easily spreads. The plant aggressively out-grows native species in ecologically sensitive areas, especially on river banks, where it can impede the flow of water at times of high rain flow, increasing the likelihood of flooding. During winter this annual dies back, leaving the bare river banks more susceptible to erosion. Himalayan balsam grows up to 2 m (6.5 feet) tall. The upright, reddish stems carry leaves in whorls of three or opposite pairs. Pink/purple flowers, 30–40 mm (1–1.5 inches) long, appear July–October.

Japanese knotweed is fast growing, reaching more than 3 m (10 feet) in height. It is quick to colonise riverbanks, roadsides and other wayside places. Large, triangular leaves are borne on red, zigzag stems. Loose spikes of white flowers arise from leaf bases and appear between August and October. Once established, populations are extremely persistent, can survive severe floods and are difficult and expensive to eradicate.

Killer shrimp The shrimp, which can grow to 3.2 cm (1¼ in), is larger than our native freshwater species and can be identified by its tiger stripes and the horns on its tail. It originates from the Black and Caspian Seas in Eastern Europe and has spread across most of Western Europe over the last ten years. *Dikerogammarus villosus* is an aggressive hunter, feeding on damselflies, small fish, water boatmen and native freshwater shrimp, threatening the Broads eco-system. It was first found in Barton Broad in March 2012 and since then it has been discovered in the River Ant at Dilham – in the Bure – from Wroxham to Acle and in the Thurne at Potter Heigham. They often move by hitching lifts on boats and fishing equipment and water users are urged to follow the **Check, Clean, Dry** campaign to help prevent its spread to other waterways. This advises river users to routinely check their equipment, including boats, clothing, and fishing gear that has been in contact with the water. They should wash it, return any organisms to the water they came from, and dry out the equipment for at least 48 hours as the shrimps can survive for several days in damp conditions. Anglers are asked not to use keep nets as shrimps tend to gather in them.

Zebra mussels are native to south east Russia. The female mussels can produce a million eggs per season, and dense colonies quickly become established which can contain hundreds of thousands of individuals. The distinctively striped mussels grow to around 30–50 mm (1–2 inches). Unlike our native mussels which burrow in sediment, the zebra mussels attach themselves to submerged hard surfaces such as pipework, masonry, lock gates and posts, and rapidly filter out nutrients from the water.

PLACES TO VISIT

There are many wonderful places to visit in the Broads, including restored windmills, ancient buildings, beautiful gardens and, of course, the Broads themselves. Listed below is just a selection – for more ideas on days out and places to go, visit one of the Broads Authority Information Centres (see Where to Get More Information, page 24). Please note that opening times are subject to change and it is always advisable to check in advance. Note that some post codes, particularly those given for nature reserves and the like, will only be the **nearest** post code to the location.

The Broads is a wetland, so for some visits you may need waterproof shoes or boots. In summer don't forget sunscreen and a sun hat. Insect repellent may be useful, especially when close to the water.

HISTORIC BUILDINGS

Bungay Castle (page 63) *6 Cross Street, Bungay, Suffolk NR35 1AU (01502 633600; www.bungay-suffolk.co.uk)* The original Norman keep was completed in 1165. A second castle was built in 1294 and this construction provided the town with the huge protective flint walls and the twin towers of the gatehouse, which can be seen today. Tourist information and visitor centre, café. *Open all year, daily 10.00–16.00; occasional evening openings, telephone for details. Donations welcome.*

Burgh Castle (page 60) *At the far western end of Breydon Water, 5 km (3 miles) west of Great Yarmouth, Norfolk NR31 9QG (0870 333 1181; www.english-heritage. org.uk; www.norfarchtrust.org.uk).* In a striking position, with panoramic views over Breydon Water. The castle comprises the imposing flint walls of a 3rd-century Roman fort, built to defend the coast from Saxon raiders. The adjacent reed beds attract many different birds, including bearded tits, reed and sedge warblers. *Access at all reasonable times. Free.*

Caister Roman Site (page 55) *Near Caister-on-Sea, 5 km (3 miles) north of Great Yarmouth, Norfolk NR30 5RN (0870 333 1181; www.english-heritage.org.uk; www. norfarchtrust.org.uk).* Remains of a Roman Saxon shore fort, including foundations and sections of wall and ditch. The fort was constructed around AD 200 and occupied until the end of the 4th century. Well-behaved dogs welcome. *Access at all reasonable times. Free.*

Norwich Castle, Museum and Art Gallery (page 49) 24 Castle Meadow, Norwich, Norfolk NR1 3JU *(01603 493649; www.museums.norfolk.gov.uk/Visit_Us/ Norwich_Castle/index.htm).* Built by the Normans as a royal palace and used as prison from the 14th century. Today the castle contains fine collections of art, archaeology and natural history, and the world's largest collection of ceramic teapots. Visitors can also discover what life was like in the Norman keep. Shop and café. Wheelchair access and disabled toilet. *Open all year, Mon–Sat 10.00–17.00 & Sun 13.00– 17.00. Closes at 16.30 in the winter. Charge.*

Norwich Cathedral (page 49) *65 The Close, Norwich, Norfolk NR1 4DH (01603 218300; www.cathedral.org.uk).* Founded in 1096 and built in the Romanesque style. It has been voted Norfolk's most loved building. The cathedral has the second tallest spire and the largest monastic cloisters in England, many of the buildings retaining their medieval origins. The herb garden is a pleasant, quiet space. Restaurant/coffee shop. Wheelchair access and disabled toilet. *Cathedral open daily 07.30–18.00; restaurant Mon–Sat 10.00–17.00, Sun 11.00–17.00; garden, daily 09.00–17.00; shop Mon–Sat 09.15–17.00, Sun 11.45–15.30. Free.*

St Benet's Abbey (page 44) *Most easily accessed by boat. By car or foot, access via a farm lane near Ludham Hall Farm, on the edge of the River Bure, Norfolk NR29 5NU (www.stbenetsabbey.org).* An isolated spot on an island called Cow Holm, beside the River Bure. A derelict 18th-century windmill and the ruins of a Benedictine monastery. *Access at all reasonable times. Free.*

St Helen's Church, Ranworth (page 43) *Ranworth, Norfolk NR13 6HS (01603 270279; www.broadsideparishes.org.uk)* Built in 1370 on the site of a Saxon church. St Helen's is known as the 'Cathedral of the Broads' and contains some wonderful treasures, including an extensive 15th-century painted rood screen and the Ranworth Antiphonal, a beautifully illuminated 15th-century service book. Climb the 30.5 m (100 feet) Ranworth tower for panoramic views of the Broads. Visitor centre (small charge) and tearoom. *Open daily during daylight hours. Free.*

St Olaves Priory (page 59) *9 km (5.5 miles) south west of Great Yarmouth, near Haddiscoe, Norfolk NR31 9HE (01493 488609; www.english-heritage.org.uk).* The rare remains of a 14th-century Augustinian priory, later a cottage occupied until 1902, located near the bridge on the banks of the River Waveney. Key available from Priory House (*see* telephone number above). Dogs on leads and only in restricted areas. *Access at all reasonable times. Free.*

Somerleyton Hall (page 60) *Lowestoft, Suffolk NR32 5QQ (0871 222 4244; www.somerleyton.co.uk).* Widely regarded as one of the best examples of a Tudor-Jacobean manor house, rebuilt in 1844 and still in use as a family home. Gardens, maze and miniature railway. All areas of the hall and gardens are wheelchair accessible. Wheelchairs available for visitors' use. Disabled toilet. Part of the Somerleyton Estate, which also includes Fritton Lake (*see* also page 94). *Open Apr-Sep Halls and Gardens open Tue, Thu, Sun & B Hols 10.00 -17.00 Gardens ONLY open on Wed. Charge.*

Waxham Great Barn (page 40) *Sea Palling, Norfolk NR12 0EE (01603 629048; www.norfolkhistoricbuildingtrust.org.uk/ projects/past/028_waxham_great_barn. htm).* A Grade I listed barn, originally constructed in the late 16th century, with later additions. Much of the building material was reused from dissolved monasteries. It is the largest barn in Norfolk, at almost 55 m (180 feet) long. Café. Wheelchair access (gravel path) and disabled toilet. *Open Apr-Oct 09.30-17.00. Café closed Wed outside school holidays. (telephone to confirm times).*

St Benet's Abbey.

🏭 MILLS AND WIND PUMPS

Berney Arms Mill (page 54) *On the north bank of the River Yare, 5.5 km (3.5 miles) north east of Reedham, Norfolk NR30 1SB (01493 700645; www.english-heritage. org. uk). Access by boat trips from Haven Bridge, Great Yarmouth; by train from Berney Arms Station; footpaths from Halverage and Great Yarmouth.* The tallest wind pump in the country, giving wonderful views of the marshes. Built to grind a constituent of cement and in use until 1951. *Access to mill by pre-booked tour, telephone to confirm times. Charge.*

Herringfleet (page 60) *South west of Herringfleet church, on the River Waveney, Suffolk NR32 5QT. Can be reached via a footpath from the B1074 (01473 264755; www.suffolkmills.org.uk/windmills/ herringfleet.html).* Constructed in the early 19th century, the mill was in use until around 1956 and is the only full-sized working smock drainage mill in the Broads. *Telephone for opening times.*

Horsey Wind Pump (page 45) *Horsey, Great Yarmouth, Norfolk NR29 4EE (01263 740241; www.nationaltrust.org.uk).* A four-storey wind pump, built in 1912, located in a great area for birdwatching. Fine views across the Broads. Wheelchair accessible nature garden, including raised ponds and wildflower meadow, and National Trust shop and tea room *open 12.00-16.30.*

Polkey's and Cadge's Mills (page 59) *NR13 3UB (01362 869394; amanda.rix@ norfolk.gov.uk; www.norfolkwindmills. co.uk). Leave A146 at Hales on Ferry Road to Reedham. Then by boat, or walk from Reedham via Wherryman's Way. Or take a train to Berney Arms and then walk to Reedham passing the site on the way. No vehicular access. Grid reference: TG 446 036.* Two drainage mills out of an original cluster of three, situated close to Seven Mile House. Polkey's Mill was built sometime prior to 1880 and is now fully restored. Now brick, but the old cap is retained. The mill drove a scoop-wheel (a paddle wheel in a brick channel), which lifted the water from the marshes, through a hinged gate, into the river. Cadge's Mill is minus cap and sails. It was also built around 1880 and last worked in 1941. The site also includes Reedham Marsh Steam Engine House and the restored Seven Mile Ruston diesel pumping engines. *Telephone for opening times.*

Stracey Arms Wind Pump (page 54) *Beside the River Bure, on A47 between Acle and Great Yarmouth, Norfolk NR13 3QE*

Thurne Dyke.

(01362 869394; amanda.rix@norfolk.gov.uk; www.norfolkwindmills.co.uk).A wind pump, originally built in 1883. *Telephone for opening times. Charge.*

Thurne Dyke (page 44) *On the River Thurne. The Staithe, Thurne, Great Yarmouth, Norfolk NR29 3BU (07796 407864) Contact debranicholson@windengines.com.* A white-painted brick tower mill, built in 1820 as a two-storey mill, with a third storey added later. The mill is complete with its sails and internal machinery. *Telephone for details. Charge.*

🏛 MUSEUMS

Beccles & District Museum (page 65) *Leman House, Ballygate, Beccles, Suffolk NR34 9ND (01502 715722 ; www.becclesmuseum.org.uk).* Housed in a magnificent 16th-century building, built in the early 1500s and restored and modernised in the 1760s. This local and natural history museum is manned entirely by unpaid volunteers. Displays range from a few Iron Age and Roman items to a large number of Victorian artifacts, including a scale model of 1854 Beccles. Large historical photographic collection of local people and places and a growing historical database of Beccles clock makers. Wheelchair access and disabled toilet. *Open Apr-Oct, Tue-Sun & B Hol Mon 13.45-16.30. Will open outside normal hours for groups and school visits: enquire in advance. Free (donation appreciated).*

Bungay Museum (page 63) *Waveney District Council Office, Broad Street, Bungay, Suffolk NR35 1EE (01986 896788: www.bungay-suffolk.co.uk).* Local history museum currently housed on the first floor of the Waveney District Council office. The collections include a large number of coins and medals, archaeological specimens, photographs, displays on local printing works, costume and textiles, decorative and applied art and social history. *Open all year, Mon-Fri 09.00-13.00 & 14.00-16.30 (closed B Hols). Charge.*

Caister Castle and Car Collection (page 55) *Castle Lane, Caister-on-Sea, Great Yarmouth, Norfolk NR30 5SN (01664 567707; www.caistercastle.co.uk).* A ruined, moated 15th-century castle, originally commissioned in 1432. The 27.5 m (90 feet) tower is intact and visitors can climb it for magnificent views. The car collection includes many rare cars and motorbikes. Also bicycles, horse-drawn vehicles and pedal cars. Picnic area, café, woodland walk. Wheelchair access and disabled toilet. *Open May-Sep, Sun-Fri 10.00-16.30. Charge (children under 5 free).*

East Anglia Transport Museum (page 66) *Chapel Road, Carlton Colville, Lowestoft, Suffolk NR33 8BL (01502 518459; www.eatm.org.uk).* A museum of street transport, based around a re-created street scene of houses and shops, with vintage commercial vehicles, buses, trams and trolley buses, cars and a light railway. Visitors can take rides on different vehicles. Exhibition halls. Regular special events. Picnic area, woodland walk, gift shop and tearooms. Well-behaved dogs welcome. Wheelchair access to many buildings, although much of the museum site has uneven terrain; wheelchair accessible tram and train – confirm availability in advance. Disabled toilet. *Opening times vary so telephone for details.*

Lowestoft Museum (page 67) *Broad House, Nicholas Everitt Park, Oulton Broad, Lowestoft, Suffolk NR33 9JR (01502 511457; www.lowestoftmuseum.org).* Housed in a 17th-C, Grade II listed building, the museum is home to an important collection of 18th-C Lowestoft Porcelain; locally found fossils and artifacts and depictions of period room settings; local industry and people associated with the town, including Benjamin Brittain. *Open daily, Apr-Oct, 13.00-16.00. Free.*

Museum of the Broads *Staithe Road, Stalham, Norwich NR12 9DA (01692 581681; www.museumofthebroads.org.uk).* An independent museum located at the historic and picturesque Stalham Staithe,

offering a view of Broadlands life. Family-friendly trails and activities for children, together with trips on the steam boat *Falcon (Tue, Wed & Thu). Open Jul-Sep, Sun-Fri 10.00-16.30, Sat 10.00-13.00. & Oct, Sun-Thu 10.00-16.00 & Sat 10.00-13.00.*

RAF Air Defence Radar Museum
(page 43) *RAF Neatishead, near Horning, Norwich, Norfolk NR12 8YB (01692 631485; www.radarmuseum.co.uk).* An award-winning museum illustrating the history and development of air defence radar since its invention in 1935, located on an operational RAF base. Visitors can explore the history and development of detection, air intelligence photography, radar and air battle management, from the 1930s through to today's computer technology. Lots of hands-on exhibits and re-created operation's room. Free guided tours, souvenir shop, café and picnic areas. Wheelchair access. *Open Apr-Oct, Tue and Thu 10.00-17.00; also the second Sat of the month all year, and B Hol Mon. Charge (children under 7 free).*

Stalham Old Firehouse Museum (page 39) *Corner of St Mary's churchyard, High Street, Stalham, Norwich, Norfolk NR12 9AZ (01692 582781; www.enjoythebroads. com/things-to-do/stalham-old-firehouse-museum).* Photographs, artefacts and a 1902 horse-drawn fire engine housed in the country's second oldest firehouse. Disabled access. *Open Easter-Sep, Tue, Thu-Fri 10.00-12.00 and 14.00-16.00 and 14.00-16.00 (telephone to check opening times and to arrange a visit). Free (donations welcome).*

Strumpshaw Steam Museum (page 52) *Old Hall, Strumpshaw , Norwich, Norfolk NR13 4HR (01603 714535; www. strumpshawsteammuseum.co.uk).* Many, many steam engines, including wagons, pumps, engines, tractors, working beam engines and a Christie cinema organ. Narrow gauge railway, a 1930s fairground, countryside walks and a collection of rare breeds. Engines in steam *last Sun in month. Annual* steam rally *end May.*

Tearoom and gift shop. Wheelchair access and toilet. Well-behaved dogs welcome. *Open Apr-Sep, Sun & B Hols 10.30-15.30. Charge.*

Time and Tide (page 55) *Blackfriars Road, Great Yarmouth, Norfolk NR30 3BX (01493 743930; www.museums.norfolk.gov.uk).* Award-winning museum housed in a converted Victorian herring-curing works. Lively exhibits describe Great Yarmouth's history and rich maritime and fishing heritage. Recreations of a Victorian fisherman's cottage, 1950s quayside and the wheelroom of a coastal drifter. Historic fishing boats and hands-on games, puzzles and children's activities. Café. Wheelchair access and toilets. *Open Apr-Oct daily 10.00-16.30; Nov-Mar, Mon-Fri 10.00-16.00, Sat-Sun 12.00-16.00. Charge.*

Toad Hole Cottage Museum (page 44) *How Hill National Nature Reserve, Ludham, Great Yarmouth, Norfolk NR29 5PG (01692 678763; www.visitthebroads.co.uk).* Situated on a nature reserve beside the River Ant. A tiny marshman's cottage, built sometime between 1780 and 1820, illustrating a home and working life on the marshes over 100 years ago. *Open Apr-May and Oct, Mon-Fri 10.30-13.00 and 13.30-17.00, weekends 10.30-17.00; Jun-Sep, daily 09.30-17.00. Free.*

⬩ NATURE RESERVES

The many nature reserves in the Broads are mostly good areas for walking as well as an opportunity to enjoy the traditional Broads landscapes and the wildlife that live there. Dogs are allowed on public rights of way under close control, but many nature reserves do not allow access for dogs. The nature reserves are generally *open daily.*

Alderfen Broad (page 43) *Near Neatishead, 3 km (2 miles) east of Hoveton, Norfolk NR12 8XT (telephone 01603 625540; www.norfolkwildlifetrust.org.uk).* Water lilies, wildfowl, dragonflies and damselflies. Footpaths around the reserve and a boardwalk to the water's edge. Muddy paths all year round.

Ant Broads and Marshes (page 39) *Close to the villages of Irstead, Barton Turf and Neatishead, on the A1151, Norfolk NR29 5DD (0300 060 1991; www.naturalengland. org.uk).* Wildfowl, fen and woodland. One of the best examples of unpolluted valley fen in western Europe. Circular boardwalk near Irstead.

Barton Broad (page 39)
Near Neatishead, 2 km (1 mile) north of Hoveton, Norfolk NR12 8XP (01603 625540; www.norfolkwildlifetrust.org.uk). The second largest broad and site of the Millennium project, Clearwater 2000, which has restored the water quality and landscape of the broad. Wheelchair access and disabled toilet.

Breydon Water and Berney Marshes
(pages 55 and 54) *Near Halvergate and Great Yarmouth (no access by road), part of the Halvergate Marshes area, access by train from Norwich or Great Yarmouth (Berney Arms Station) or by footpath from Halvergate or Great Yarmouth, Norfolk NR31 9HU (01493 700645; www.rspb.org.uk).* Breydon Water is the confluence of the Rivers Yare and Waveney, before they join the River Bure. Visitors can see geese, ducks and waders. Berney Marshes is a huge expanse of grazing marsh, home to thousands of ducks, geese and swans in winter, and lapwings and redshanks in the spring.

Broads Wildlife Centre (page 43) *On Ranworth Broad, signposted from B1140 at South Walsham, Norfolk NR13 6HY (01603 270479; www.norfolkwildlifetrust.org.uk).* This floating wildlife centre is situated at the end of an informative boardwalk. Ferry boat available in afternoons, *Apr–Oct only*. Fabulous views from the centre, where there are interactive displays and children's activities. Refreshments available. Wheelchair access and disabled toilet. *The nature reserve is open all year; the wildlife centre is open Apr–Oct, daily 10.00–17.00.*

Bure Marshes (page 43) Fen, broads and fen woodland. The Bure Marshes reserve lies on either side of the River Bure, between Wroxham and Ranworth. The site includes four broads: Hoveton Great Broad (*see* page 43), Decoy Broad, Ranworth Broad and Cockshoot Broad (*see* below).

Carlton Marshes (page 66) *Burnt Hill Lane, Lowestoft, Suffolk NR33 8HU (01502 564250; www.suffolkwildlife.org).* Suffolk Broads Wildlife Centre and walks across the grazing marshes. A regular haunt of wintering waders and birds of prey. Water vole can be seen among the dykes. *Regular* events, including children's activity days during school holidays. Wheelchair access and disabled toilet. Dogs on leads only. *Telephone for centre opening times.*

Sunset over Bure Marshes.

Cockshoot Broad (page 43) *Near Woodbastwick, Norfolk NR12 8BF (01603 625540; www.norfolkwildlifetrust.org. uk).* Cockshoot Broad is not navigable by own boat, public access by boat trip only to boardwalk at present. The site of a pioneering project to restore clear water for the water lily beds and damsel flies. The site of a pioneering project to restore clear water and wildlife, and renowned for the water lily beds and damselflies. Wheelchair access.

Hickling Broad (page 40) *Part of the Upper Thurne broads and marshes, approximately 4 km (2.5 miles) south of Stalham, Norfolk NR12 0BW (01692 598276; www. norfolkwildlifetrust.org.uk).* The largest expanse of open water in the Broads. There is a boarded walkway to the broad, together with walking trails, boat trips, and a visitor centre. Excellent views of raptors from the raptor roost at Stubb Mill *Oct–Mar.* Wheelchair access and disabled toilet. *Reserve open daily 10.00–17.00; visitor centre open Apr–Sep.*

Horsey Mere (page 41) *Horsey, Great Yarmouth, Norfolk NR29 4EE (01263 740241; www.nationaltrust.org.uk).* Open water, reed beds, grazing marshes and a wildfowl sanctuary. Horsey wind pump *(see page 88)* is located here and there are waymarked circular walks.

Hoveton Great Broad (page 43) *Part of Bure Marshes. No access by road, reached by water from moorings on the River Bure beside the entrance (0845 600 3078; www. naturalengland.org.uk).* A trail through woodland on the edge of the broad.

How Hill National Nature Reserve (page 44) *Near Ludham, Great Yarmouth, Norfolk NR29 5PG (01603 756096; www. visitthebroads.co.uk).* A National Nature Reserve of fen, grazing marsh and woodland. Walking trails and boat trips onboard the *Electric Eel.* There are three wind pumps on the reserve and Toad Hole Cottage Museum *(see page 90). Open Apr– May and Oct, daily 10.30–17.00; Jun–Sep, daily 09.30–18.00.*

Martham Broad (page 46) *Martham, near Winterton-on-Sea, Norfolk NR29 4EB (01603 625540; www.norfolkwildlifetrust.org.uk).* Open water, reed and sedge fen. In summer a good place to see swallowtail butterflies. Public footpaths (muddy) to the north and south.

Mid Yare Nature Reserve (page 51) *North and south of the River Yare, near Strumpshaw Fen, 5 km (3 miles) east of Norwich, Norfolk NR13 4HW (01603 661662; www.rspb.org.uk).* Fen, woodland, grazing marsh, open water, dykes and reed beds, all supporting wintering and breeding wildfowl, wigeon, marsh harriers, and butterflies, including the swallowtail. Nature trail and hides at Strumpshaw.

Oulton Marshes (page 66) *Reached by a path from Oulton Church or by water from Oulton Dyke. Church Lane Oulton, Suffolk NR32 3JP (01603 610734; www. visitthebroads.co.uk).* Grazing meadows, fen habitat and dykes and pools, with a variety of wetland plants and breeding birds.

Ranworth Broad (page 43). *Adjacent to Cockshoot Broad, Norfolk NR12 8BF (01603 625540; www.norfolkwildlifetrust.org.uk).* Access is by footpath from road to a boarded walkway, leading to the Norfolk Wildlife Trust Centre on the edge of the Broad.

Strumpshaw Fen (page 51) *On the River Yare near Brundall, Norwich, Norfolk NR13 4HS (01603 715191; www.rspb.org.uk).* Reed beds, grazing marshes, meadows and woodland. Opportunities to see marsh harriers, bitterns and kingfishers, dragonflies and butterflies, including the swallowtail. Walking trails (muddy and wet in winter) and hides. Wheelchair access and disabled toilet.

Surlingham Church Marsh (page 51) *Near Surlingham Church, Norwich, Norfolk NR14 7DF (01603 715191; www.rspb.org.uk).* A former grazing marsh with pools, dykes and summer marsh and meadow flowers. Marsh harriers, kingfishers, water rails, and reed and sedge warblers may be seen. Circular walk and bird hides.

Upton Fen (page 44) *North of Acle off the A47, near Upton Broad, Norfolk NR29 3BT (01603 625540; www.wildlifetrust.org.uk).* Walks through tangled fen and woodland. Marsh harrier and water vole can be seen all year round and the fen is also a good place to see dragonflies. Waymarked trail (muddy all year) and boardwalk.

Ted Ellis Nature Reserve (page 57) *Wheatfen Broad, The Covey, off The Green, Surlingham, Norwich, Norfolk NR14 7AL (01508 538036; www.wheatfen.org).* Ted Ellis was a writer and broacaster who lived at Wheatfen Broad for 40 years. Wheatfen Broad is one of the last tidal marshes of the once extensive swamp area of the Yare Valley, and is an extremely sensitive site. Events throughout the year (see website). Some paths suitable for wheelchairs.

Winterton Dunes (page 46) *Near Winterton-on-Sea, Norfolk NR29 4AS (0845 600 3078; www.naturalengland.org.uk).* Dunes, heath, grassland, birch woodland and beach. This area is unusual because it has great ecological similarities to the dune systems of the Baltic rather than the geographically closer dunes along the Norfolk Coast. Natterjack toads breed in pools, which are also used by dragonflies. Many different species of breeding and over-wintering birds can be seen. Refreshments, toilets and parking available at Winterton-on-Sea car park.

★ OTHER PLACES TO VISIT

BeWILDerwood (page 43) *Horning Road, Hoveton, Norfolk NR12 8JW (01692 633033; www.bewilderwood.co.uk).* A wild and imaginative adventure park for both children and grown ups, with treehouses, zip wires, jungle bridges, boat trips and marsh walks. It is the setting for the children's book *A Boggle at BeWILDerwood*, by local author Tom Blofeld. Broadland Cycle Hire (*see* page 71) offers bike hire from the car park. Meals and snacks available. Picnic areas and lots of seating. Disabled play equipment and facilities but upper woodland area is naturally sloping and may be difficult to access. Guide dogs

only. *Open daily 10.00–17.30 or dusk if earlier, please check before visiting. Charge.*

Barton House Railway (page 42) *Hartwell Road, The Avenue, Wroxham, Norfolk NR12 8TL 01603 782008; www.bartonhouserailway.org.uk).* The golden age of the steam railway is re-created at this site beside the River Bure, with two ride-on railways, authentic tickets and museum of railway artefacts. The signal box was originally built in 1901 at Honing Station, and visitors can watch the signalman at work. Home baking and light meals. *Open Apr–Oct, 3rd Sun in every month and Easter Mon, 14.30–17.30. Charge.*

Bure Valley Railway (Wroxham page 52) *Aylsham Station, Norwich Road, Aylsham, Norfolk NR11 6BW (01263 733858; www.bvrw.co.uk).* Narrow gauge railway running both steam and diesel locomotives between Aylsham and Wroxham, with connections to Broads boat trips at Wroxham (maximum of two dogs allowed per boat). The railway runs alongside the Bure Valley cycle and footpath, and cycles can be carried aboard scheduled services. Restaurant and souvenir shop. Wheelchair access to Aylsham and Wroxham stations, including shops, toilets, café, platforms and Aylsham workshops; specially designed coaches accommodate wheelchairs; disabled toilet. Well behaved dogs welcome. *Open Easter–Oct, telephone or visit website for timetable. Charge.*

Fairhaven Woodland & Water Garden (page 44) *School Road, South Walsham, Norfolk NR13 6DZ (01603 270449/270683; www.fairhavengarden.co.uk).* 131 acres of ancient woodland, water gardens and a private broad, described as a garden for all seasons. Tea-room (*see* Eating Out, page 29), children's trail, plant sales and boat trips. Wheelchair access to 90 per cent of gardens (including boat trips), mobility scooters available to borrow, disabled toilet. *Open daily Mar–Nov 10.00–17.00 & Dec–Feb 10.00-16.00; also May-Aug, Wed–Thu until 21.00. Charge.*

Fritton Lake (page 60) *Beccles Road, Fritton, Great Yarmouth, Norfolk NR31 9HA (0333 456 0777; www.frittonlakeoc.co.uk).* Boat trips and rowing boats for hire, children's activities including indoor barn games and a Viking fort, gardens (including a maze) and nature trails, swimming, golf, fishing and pony rides. The lake forms part of Somerleyton Estate which encompasses Somerleyton Hall (*see* page 87). Pub and tearoom. All areas of the hall and gardens are wheelchair accessible, and there is a *Wheelyboat* (advanced booking essential) for disabled use. Disabled toilet. *Opening times vary so telephone for details – similar to Somerleyton Hall page 87).*

Great Yarmouth Row Houses (page 55) *111 South Quay, Great Yarmouth, Norfolk NR30 2RG (01493 857900; www.english-heritage.org.uk).* The narrow lanes of the Yarmouth Rows, a feature of the older part of the town, were originally a network of alleyways connecting the dwellings crammed inside Yarmouth's town walls. Many of the Row houses were damaged by World War II bombing or demolished after the war, but these surviving dwellings have been restored as fascinating museums. *Open Apr–Sep, daily 12.00–17.00. Charge.*

Hoveton Hall Gardens (page 43) *1.5 km (1 mile) north of Wroxham, Norwich, Norfolk NR12 8RJ (01603 782558; www.hovetonhallgardens.co.uk).* A delightful 6 hectares (15 acres) of woodland and walled gardens, water garden and lake. Tearoom and plant sales. Majority of the gardens are suitable for wheelchair access. Guide dogs only. *Open Apr–Sep, 10.30–17.00 Sun–Fri. Telephone or check website before visiting. Charge.*

Pettitts Animal Adventure Park (page 59) *Church Road, Reedham, Norfolk NR13 3UA (01493 700094; www.pettittsadventurepark.co.uk).* Exotic and domestic animals and birds, animals to feed, children's rides, magic and clown shows. Café and snack bar with picnic benches designed with wheelchairs and buggies in mind. Wheelchair access and disabled toilet. *Open Apr–Oct, daily 10.00–17.00. Charge.*

Pleasurewood Hills (page 67) *Leisure Way, Corton, Lowestoft, Suffolk NR32 5DZ (01502 586000; www.pleasurewoodhills.co.uk).* An award-winning theme park. Thrill rides and white-water adventures, including the tallest rollercoaster in the east of England. Also shows, less

Pleasurewood Hills.

demanding family rides and a miniature railway. Tearooms. Disabled access. *Opening times revolve around the school holidays so visit the website or telephone for full details.*

Sea Life Centre (page 55) *Marine Parade, Great Yarmouth, Norfolk NR30 3AH (01493 330631; www.sealife.co.uk).* Many native species and a tropical ocean display. Visitors can eyeball all kinds of underwater creatures, from shrimps to sharks. Wheelchair access and disabled toilet. *Open all year, daily from 10.00, except Xmas & Boxing day. Closing times vary from 15.00-17.00 so check the website or telephone for details. Charge.*

Thrigby Hall Wildlife Gardens (page 54) *Filby, near Great Yarmouth, Norfolk NR29 3DR (01493 369477; www.thrigbyhall. co.uk).* Beautifully landscaped gardens and a specialised collection of animals, birds and reptiles. Attractions include a Willow Pattern Garden, Lime Tree Lookout and the Tiger Tree Walkway constructed in the tree tops above the tigers' enclosure. Wheelchair access and disabled toilet. *Open all year, daily from 10.00. Parking and children's play areas free, charge for admission to Wildlife Gardens.*

Whitlingham Country Park (page 50) *Whitlingham Lane, near Trowse, Norwich NR14 8TR (01603 632307; www. charitabletrust.com;www.visitthebroads. co.uk).* Beautiful countryside with two broads, woodland and meadows, beside the River Yare. The solar boat *Ra* operates here for a high-tech experience of the Great Broad. Walking and cycling trails, bird watching, visitor centre, solar boat trips and café. The Whitlingham Outdoor Education Centre is located here and offers a wide range of land and water based activities including sailing, windsurfing, climbing and archery. Wheelchair access and disabled toilet. All terrain wheelchairs available for loan, telephone *01603 617332* to book. *Open all year, daily. Admission free, charge for activities.*

Wroxham Barns (page 42) *Tunstead Road, Hoveton, Norfolk NR12 8QU (01603 783762; www.wroxhambarns.co.uk).* Craft studios, plant centre, farmers' market, children's farm and funfair, all set in and around restored barns and agricultural buildings. Restaurant. Wheelchair access and disabled toilet. Guide dogs only. *Open all year, daily 10.00-17.00. Admission free. Charge for children's farm and funfair (children under two go free).*

ACKNOWLEDGEMENTS

Photographs marked BA are reproduced by kind permission of the Broads Authority.
Photographs marked NNSS are © Crown Copyright 2009, GB Non-Native Species Secretariat.
Photographs marked FGT are reproduced by kind permission of the Fairhaven Gardens Trust.
Photographs marked S courtesy of Shutterstock.

3, S, Ian Dyball; 4, S, Helen Hotson; 5-7 corners, S, Laurence Gough; 6, S, Helen Hotson; 8, BA; 9-13 corners, S, Joy Fera; 9, Jonathan Mosse; 12, David Burton / Alamy Stock Photo; 15-17 corners, S, Paul Cowan; 17, Clive Tully / Alamy Stock Photo; 19 corner, S, Stephen Finn; 20 S, Christopher Elwell; 21-23 corners, S, maga; 21, BA; 22, foopath sign, S, Mark William Richardson; 22, Broads walk sign, BA; 23, S, Helen Hotson; 25-27 corners, S, northallertonman; 29-35 S Neil Langan; 33 Shepps / Shutterstock.com; 35-37 corners, S, Laurence Gough; 37, S, Paul Cowan; 39-69 corners, S, Meirion Matthias; 41, S, David Hughes; 47, S, Andrew Howard; 48, S, merion matthias; 52, S, Steve Bramall; 56, BA; 61, S, Mike J Roberts; 62, Adrian Muttitt / Alamy Stock Photo; 67, S,Richard Bowden; 68, S, Ian Dyball; 69, S, David Hughes; 71-75 corners, Philip Bird LRPS CPAGB / Shutterstock.com; 77-85 corners, BA; 76, BA; 77, Bearded tit, S, Cosmin Manci; 77, Bewick's swan, S, Robbie Taylor; 77, Bittern, S, Borislav Borisov; 77, Long-tailed tit, Paul Huggins; 78, Marsh harrier, S, iliuta goean; 78, Reed warbler, S, Iurii Konoval; 78, Treecreeper, S, Sue Robinson; 78, Wigeon, S, feathercollector; 78, Willow tit, S, Kristof Degreef; 79, Bream, S, Dewitt; 79, Perch, S, Krasowit; 79, Pike, S, Silvia Iordache; 79, Rudd, S, Gala_Kan; 80, Comma butterfly, S, willmetts; 80, Common darter Dragonfly, BA; 80, Banded demoiselle, Paul Huggins; 80, Glow worm, dave-pemcoastphotos.com; 80, Norfolk hawker, S, Ainars Aunins; 81, Swallowtail, S, Marek Mierzejewski, 81, Brown hare, S, Pavel Mikoska; 81, Daubentons bat, Mike Lane; 81, Harvest mouse, S, Eric Isselée; 81, Otter, S, JKlingebiel; 82, Red deer, S, Ewan Chesser; 82, Water vole, laurencea; 82, Buckler fern, S, Drahomír Kalina; 82, Cross-leaved heath, S, Ainars Aunins; 82, Early marsh orchid, S, Ainars Aunins; 83, Grey Willow, S, Cosmin Manci; 83, Guelder rose, S, Malgorzata Kistryn; 83, Ragged robin, S, Steven Paul Pepper; 83, Meadow thistle, S, RTimages; 83, Yellow water lily, S, Gregory Johnston, 84, American mink, NNSS; 84, Himalayan Balsam, NNSS; 85, Japanese knotweed, S, Steve McWilliam; 85, Killer Shrimp, BA; 85, Zebra mussels, S, David P. Lewis; 87-89 corners, S, Richard Bowden; 87, S, BMA; 88, S, Kevin Whitehouse; 91, S, Meirion Matthias; 94, Martin Charles Hatch / Shutterstock.com

INDEX

Page numbers shown in **bold** indicate map pages.

accidents 14; *see also* emergencies, incident reporting
activities, other 20-3
Alderfen Broad 90
Angles Way footpath 23
angling 20, 25
Ant Broads and Marshes **39**, 91
Ant, River 31, **38-9**, **43-5**, 70
Barton Broad 6, 19, 23 **39**, **43**, 91
Barton House Railway 93
Beccles 6, 22-23, **65**
Beccles & District Museum 89
Berney Arms Mill 33, **54**, **69**, 88
BeWILDerwood **43**, 93
boardwalks 20, 23
boat booking agencies 74
boat handling 8, 19
boat hire 4, 70-5
Boat Safety Scheme 7
boat trips 4-5, 70-5
Boater's Handbook 8-9
Boating Need to Know 8-13
boating useful contacts 25
boatyards 7-8, 11, 70-75
Breydon Bridge **55**, **68-9**
Breydon Water 11, 13, 15, **54-55**, **68-9**
Breydon Water and Berney Marshes **54-55**, 91
bridge gauge boards 14
bridge pilots 26
bridges 14-15
Broadcaster 20, 24
Broadland Churches cycle trail 22
Broads Authority 2-24
Broads Beat 19, 26
Broads Control 9, 14, 16
Broads Walks 22-23
Broads Wildlife Centre **43**, 91
Bungay Castle 86
Bungay Museum 89
Bure Marshes **43**, 91-92
Bure, River 31, **42-3**, **44-5**, **52-3**, **54-5**, 70, 72, 75, 91, 93
Bure Valley Path 22
Bure Valley Railway **42**, 93
Burgh Castle **69**, 86
Cadge's Mill **59**, 88
Caister Castle & Car Collection 89
Caister Roman Site **55**, 86
Canal and River Trust 7-8, 25-26
canoe hire 70-5
canoe training 70-75
canoeing 4, 26
carbon monoxide 7, 18-19
Carlton Marshes **66**, 91
Chet, River 31, **56-7**, 72
church services 26
Claremont Pier 67
Cockshoot Broad **43**, 91-92

Code of Conduct, Broads Authority 4
cooking outdoors 7, 10, 18
Countryside Code **38**
craft registration 6
cycle hire 21-22, 70-5
cycle routes 22
cycling 21, 22, 26
disabled access 20, 23, 25, 75
dogs 10, 18, 22, 70
drinking 19
East Anglian Transport Museum **66**, 89
Eating Out 28-33
electric boat hire 70-5
electric boats 4-5
electric charging points 8-10
Ellis, Ted 3
Ellis, Ted, Nature Reserve **51**, 93
emergencies 9; *see also* accidents, incident reporting
Environment Agency 7-11, 20, 25-26
environmentally friendly boating 10, 17
Fairhaven Woodland & Water Garden **44**, 93
Filby Broad 6-7
fire safety 18
Fritton Lake **60**, 94
fuel 10-11, 18-19
Getting Onto the Water 4-7
going aground 11
Great Yarmouth 15, **54-55**
Great Yarmouth Row Houses 94
Great Yarmouth Yacht Station 15, **68**
Green Blue, The 11, 26
Haddiscoe Cut 17, **57**
Haven Bridge 68
health 26
Herringfleet 88
Hickling Broad 5, 11, **40**, 85, 92
hire, boat 4, 70-5
hire, cycle 21, 22, 70-5
Hire, Where to 70-5
historic buildings 86-7
Horsey Mere **41**, 92
Horsey Wind Pump 45, **47**, 88
hospitals 26
Hoveton **42**
Hoveton Great Broad **43**, 92
Hoveton Hall Gardens **42**, 94
How Hill 5, 17, **44**, 92
incident reporting 15; *see also* accidents, emergencies
Information Centres, Broads Authority 20, 24
Inland Waterways Association 4, 26
invasive species 11, 26, **64**, 84-5
journey times 35
Key to Map Pages 36-37
Key to Symbols back cover flap

landscape, types of 76
launch sites *see* slipways
lavatories 11
life-jackets 11, 14, 18
Lowestoft **66-7**
Lowestoft Museum 89
Ludham Bridge 21-22, 43
Ludham Marshes **44**
Malthouse Broad **44**
maps **38-69**
Martham Broad 11, **46**, 92
Meadow Dyke **40-1**
Mid Yare Nature Reserve **51**, 92
mills and wind pumps, 88-89
mooring 11, 28
motor boat hire 70-5
motor boats 4
museums 86-90
national parks 26
nature reserves 90-3
Navigation Notes 14-17
Norfolk wherry 5
Norfolk Wherry Trust 6, **47**, **58**
Norwich 23, **48-49**
Norwich Castle, Museum and Art Gallery **48**, 86
Norwich Cathedral **48**, 86
Norwich Yacht Station **48**
Notice to Mariners 16
Oulton Marshes **66**, 92
plants 82-3
Pettitts Animal Adventure **59**, 94
Pleasurewood Hills 94
police 19, 26
Polkey's Mill **58**, 59, 88
pollution 16
Potter Heigham 15, **45**
Rangers, Broads Authority 9
Ranworth Broad 5, **43**, 92
Ranworth Staithe 5, 43
recycling 10
reed and sedge cutting 56
Reedham chain ferry 17, 56, **58**
regattas 12
Rollesby Broad **46**
rowing boat hire 70-5
RAF Air Defence Radar Museum 90
Royal Yachting Association 26
rubbish 10
rules of the road 16
safety 17-19
sailing dinghy hire 70-5
sailing schools 4, 5, 70-5
sailing yachts, dinghies 4
St Benet's Abbey 22, **44**, 86-87
St Helen's Church, Ranworth **43**, 87
St Olaves Priory **59**, 87
Salhouse Broad 4, **43**
Sealife Centre **55**, 95
slipways 6
Somerleyton Hall **60-61**, 87
South Trinity Broads Benefice cycle trail 22

speed limits 12, 30
Stalham Old Firehouse Museum 90
Stay Safe 18-19
steering 8, 19
Stracey Arms Wind Pump **54**, 88
Strumpshaw Fen **51**, 92
Strumpshaw Steam Museum 90
Suffolk Wildlife Trust **63**
Surlingham Church Marsh **51**, 92
Sustrans National Cycle Routes 22
swimming 18
Symbols, Key to back cover flap
Three Rivers Way 23
Thurne Dyke **44**, 88
Thurne Dyke Mill **44**, 47
Thurne, River 31, 45, **44-5**, **46-7**, 72, 73, 75
Time and Tide 90
tide tables 13
Toad Hole Cottage Museum **44**, 90
tolls 6-7, 13
Tourist Information Centres 24; *see also* Information Centres
training 26, *see also* sailing schools
travel 27
Trigby Hall 95
Upton Dyke **53**
Upton Fen **52**, 93
using your own craft 6
walking 22-23, 27
walks 22-3
water 13
waterskiing 13, 27, 30
waterways signs 34
Waveney, River 5, 31, **58-9**, **60-1**, **62-63**, **65**, **66-7**, 73, 74
Waxham Great Barn 40, 87
weather forecast 27
Weavers' Way footpath 23
websites 25
Weil's disease 19, 27
Wensum, River **48-9**
wheelchair access *see* disabled access
Where to Get More Information 24-27
Where to Hire 70-5
Wherryman's Way footpath 23
Wherry Maud Trust 6
Whitlingham Great and Little Broads 74
Wildlife of the Broads 76-85
wildlife rescue 27
windsurfing 5
Winterton Dunes **46**, 93
Wroxham 15, 42
Wroxham Barns **42**, 95
Yacht Stations 16
Yare, River 17, 31, **50-1**, **54-5**, **56-7**, **58-9**, 75